"*Autism in Polyvagal Terms* is a refreshingly friendly, candid, accessible, and practical read. Drawing on scientific research, engaging case studies, and personal anecdotes, the author explains that those with autism are living with a nervous system in a state of threat, and then goes on to describe a wide range of interventions guided by qualities like kindness and organicity to help this population attain a felt sense of safety. A priceless treasure for the ASD community and professionals who work with them, this book evokes a deep sense of compassion for those with autism, elucidates the source of their challenges, and offers a variety of skills to use in practice. Highly recommended!"

—**Pat Ogden,** CEO and founder of Sensorimotor
Psychotherapy Institute®

"*Autism in Polyvagal Terms* will explain why many autistic people have so much anxiety. My nervous system was reacting as if I were in a jungle surrounded by dangerous predators. This book will give therapists a framework to understand how the autistic nervous system is related to many autistic behaviors."

—**Temple Grandin,** author of *Thinking in Pictures*

"This book opens a powerful new conversation between interventions based on naturally occurring biobehavioral phenomena associated with an autonomic state of defense and a newer form of behavioral and cognitive therapy based on the psychology of mindfulness, cognitive flexibility, and emotional openness. Its methods are presented clearly but humbly, in a spirit of open examination and clinical consideration—a spirit that will help dismantle needless walls between traditions as we focus on creative new ways to advance the interests of the clients we serve. On almost every page I found interesting ideas worthy of study, exploration, and empirical examination. Highly recommended."

—**Steven C. Hayes, PhD,** Foundation Professor of
Psychology, emeritus, University of Nevada, Reno,
and originator of Acceptance and Commitment Therapy

"*Autism in Polyvagal Terms* adds an important and previously overlooked understanding of the challenges faced by autistic people and offers new insights to provide support. Sean Inderbitzen, drawing from his firsthand experiences as an autistic person informed by his expertise as a mental health professional, explains how Polyvagal Theory helps to interpret an autistic person's reactions through the lens of underlying neural mechanisms, and then provides guidance through actionable recommendations. This work is a significant, cutting-edge contribution to our current understanding of autism and promising treatment approaches."

—**Barry M. Prizant, PhD, CCC-SLP,** author of *Uniquely Human: A Different Way of Seeing Autism,* and adjunct professor, department of communicative disorders, University of Rhode Island

Autism in Polyvagal Terms

THE NORTON SERIES ON INTERPERSONAL NEUROBIOLOGY

Louis Cozolino, PhD, Series Editor
Allan N. Schore, PhD, Series Editor (2007–2014)
Daniel J. Siegel, MD, Founding Editor

The field of mental health is in a tremendously exciting period of growth and conceptual reorganization. Independent findings from a variety of scientific endeavors are converging in an interdisciplinary view of the mind and mental well-being. An interpersonal neurobiology of human development enables us to understand that the structure and function of the mind and brain are shaped by experiences, especially those involving emotional relationships.

The Norton Series on Interpersonal Neurobiology provides cutting-edge, multidisciplinary views that further our understanding of the complex neurobiology of the human mind. By drawing on a wide range of traditionally independent fields of research—such as neurobiology, genetics, memory, attachment, complex systems, anthropology, and evolutionary psychology—these texts offer mental health professionals a review and synthesis of scientific findings often inaccessible to clinicians. The books advance our understanding of human experience by finding the unity of knowledge, or consilience, that emerges with the translation of findings from numerous domains of study into a common language and conceptual framework. The series integrates the best of modern science with the healing art of psychotherapy.

AUTISM IN
POLYVAGAL
TERMS

New Possibilities
and Interventions

Sean M. Inderbitzen

Foreword by Stephen W. Porges

Norton Professional Books

An Imprint of W. W. Norton & Company
Independent Publishers Since 1923

This book is intended as a general information resource for professionals practicing in the field of psychotherapy and mental health. It is not a substitute for appropriate training or clinical supervision. Standards of clinical practice and protocol vary in different practice settings and change over time. No technique or recommendation is guaranteed to be safe or effective in all circumstances, and neither the publisher nor the author(s) can guarantee the complete accuracy, efficacy, or appropriateness of any particular recommendation in every respect or in all settings or circumstances.

Any URLs displayed in this book link or refer to websites that existed as of press time. The publisher is not responsible for, and should not be deemed to endorse or recommend, any website other than its own or any content that it did not create. The author, also, is not responsible for any third-party material.

CONTENTS

ACKNOWLEDGMENTS

I dedicate this text to my boys, Shiloh and Bohannan, without whom the strength to stick around and figure out my calling never would have been possible.

Thanks to Erin Yilmaz for editing my earliest drafts and giving me feedback when others didn't think this work was possible. I don't know if I would have kept trying without you.

To Dr. Stephen Porges, and his work in Polyvagal Theory and his friendship, without whom we wouldn't be able to think differently about autism.

To Dr. Barry Prizant, for believing in me well before I could see how talented I was—your faith in me does not go unnoticed.

To my friends at Different Brains (Joseph Satchi and Hackie Reitman) for offering me opportunities to share my vision and ideas before anyone else did.

To Susan Kettler, without whom I never would have survived as a therapist. You gave some of the best clinical supervision one could hope to have, and the freedom to explore my own ability to do therapy.

To Cyndi Cathey, who believes in me and has taken more chances to advocate for me than I might ever have for myself.

To Katie Diebold, whose partnership in research on psychotherapy practice in autism makes my wild ideas possible, and whose friendship is so appreciated.

To my mother, who always told me, "I hope you dance," so I've never really stopped.

To my best friend, Kat Groff. You always said to me, "Be kinder to my friend Sean"—I've not forgotten that, and here's a book to honor that request.

FOREWORD

Writing the foreword for *Autism in Polyvagal Terms* has provided an opportunity to review aspects of my research history that touched on autism. During the 50 plus years that I have been an academic researcher, interest in autism has changed, and so has public awareness. The domain of research in and treatment of autism has not followed a linear pattern, in which research findings have led to advancements in treatments and optimized outcomes. Rather, from my perspective, the trajectory has been one of misguided research priorities based on faulty assumptions of causality of a diverse phenotype that is greatly influenced by potentially transitory state changes. This sequence of academic biases has had a profound consequence for the autism community, by limiting development of alternative models of the disorder. Potentially, alternative strategies would lead to tools that would optimize quality of life for individuals with autism and lessen the burden of the diagnosis on these individuals and their families, caregivers, and schools.

This book, consistent with Polyvagal Theory, presents an optimistic perspective for those with autism and those who support their personal journey. This perspective emphasizes that many of the features of autism may not be locked to a genetic unfolding; rather, they may depend on adaptive autonomic reactions to threat. By moving the causal model from genes to autonomic state, clinically relevant questions move from genetic screening, with an unfulfilled promise of remediation, to neural exercises that can functionally rebuild autonomic-state flexibility and resilience. For example, in this book Dr. Sean Inderbitzen proposes neural exercises that challenge autonomic regulation via withdrawing and reengaging the vagal brake, which would promote a general enhanced state of regulation observable in behavior, emotion, and physiology.

When I started my academic career in 1970, autism was considered a relatively rare disorder that was assumed to be characterized by two features: (1) permanence of the disorder and (2) a genetic basis. These plausible assumptions biased and limited the research questions and the explanations that both researchers and clinicians could use to describe their observations, in both the laboratory and the clinic. The scientific community, as well as my first publication mentioning autism (Porges, 1976), readily embraced these assumptions, which had consequences on research funding. Funding priorities within the National Institute of Mental Health reflected this transition, prioritizing projects involving molecular genetics in a concerted effort to identify a genetic substrate. This diverted funds from other, more flexible, optimistic perspectives that might be conceptualized as neural exercises to optimize the life experiences of those with an autism diagnosis. This decision was costly to the science of understanding autism and to the autism community.

Under these assumptions, when clinicians and researchers observed that an individual, via maturation or intervention, no longer reached criteria for autism, they were confronted with the consensus view that the initial diagnosis was faulty. This perspective had great impact on intervention models, interpretations of research findings, and even the astute observations of clinicians who were effective in optimizing the function of their autistic clients. Explaining to colleagues or parents that an individual no longer reached diagnostic criteria following an intervention, or with maturation, challenged clinical researchers in how to disseminate this information. If they proposed that the intervention functionally "normalized" the previously diagnosed autistic individual, then they could be accused of claiming to "cure" autism. Such a label would be sufficient to exclude a researcher from opportunities to publish in peer-reviewed journals and from obtaining funding from the National Institutes of Health, and could even impede career advancement (e.g., university tenure). Yet, within the community of researchers and clinicians, there were frequent discussions of possible explanations for shifts in severity of autistic symptoms.

The first potential source of variation in clinical sequelae was diagnosis. Thus, it was assumed that if the community studying and treating autism used a common diagnostic tool, there would be more consistency in diagnosis. This should lead both to fewer false positives (those who reverse symptoms through maturation and intervention) and to systematic evaluations of interventions reputed to "normalize" autistic behaviors. In the 1990s transformative research headed by Dr. Catherine Lord established a convergence between assessment tools and consensus of expert clinicians. These tools, the AUTISM DIAGNOSTIC OBSERVATION SCHEDULE (ADOS AND ADOS-2) and the AUTISM DIAGNOSTIC INTERVIEW (ADI

AND ADI-R), are considered the "gold standard" for diagnosing autism (Lord et al., 1993, 1999) and have led to the more inclusive diagnostic category AUTISM SPECTRUM DISORDER (ASD). The availability of these assessments framed peer-reviewed research on autism and became an important criterion to publish and receive funding. However—and this is crucial—this strategy assumed that consensus judgment was sufficient to operationalize diagnosis. This is a powerful assumption: that the behaviors observed by clinicians were sufficient to identify a disorder assumed to be genetic, or at least to have a permanent neurobiological substrate. This assumption, in practice, depends on accepting that biology and physiology parallel psychology—which often is not the case.

This model of parallelism, which assumes continuity across neural, physiological, behavioral, and psychological domains, has led to faulty inferences by assuming that variations in the expressed psychological and behavioral symptoms indexed by the ADOS and ADI would accurately map to the variations in neurobiology assumed to underlie autism. Research programs were initiated and funded that assumed standardized diagnostic tools would lead to greater understanding of underlying mechanisms. However, this inquiry made a powerful yet unsubstantiated assumption: that defining a phenotype via clinical observations (phenomenological data) would uncover mechanistic neurobiological pathways that lead to the diagnosis. Although phenotype provides essential information about an individual's observable traits, it is not sufficient to accurately identify the underlying genotype, because genetics is highly complex, and phenotype can also be influenced by environment, as well as genetic variation and epigenetic influences. At present, given the variations in phenotype, DNA sequencing has identified only a few genetic markers that correlate to increased prevalence of an autism diagnosis, but it has not provided a more definitive model that would lead to genetic mapping of autism.

In a sense, psychophysiological parallelism implicitly assumed, optimistically, that if the constructs employed in different domains (e.g., subjective, observable, physiological) were valid, and if they focused on establishing correlations across domains, this would lead to an objectively quantifiable, physiological signature of the psychological construct of autism—an assumption that has borne little fruit. There also has been fervent interest in applying imaging technologies to monitor cortical processes and to identify a brain signature (e.g., connectivity pattern) that would lead to an objective metric of brain function to support a "functional" diagnosis of autism, which has also been unsuccessful.

Although Polyvagal Theory (Porges, 1995) emerged from traditional psycho-physiology, it provides a theoretical demarcation from this assumption of parallelism. Polyvagal Theory emphasizes the interactive and integrative aspect of different levels of the nervous system that are expressed as autonomic states. The theory posits a hierarchical organization that mirrors phylogenetic shifts among vertebrates. The evolutionary changes are also reflected in maturational trends. Thus, what appears to be more complex and related to higher brain structures, such as language and sensitivities to another's physiological state via intonation of voice and gesture, reflects the functional and structural changes mapped to the evolutionary history of vertebrates. Our cortical-centric and cognitive-centric orientation can blind us to autistic features linked to older brain mechanisms that manage our basic survival-oriented reactions. Although the less complex, earlier evolved systems are often repurposed in mammals, they remain survival oriented and are efficiently available to support states of defense when survival is challenged. The hierarchical nature of the nervous system recruits foundational survival systems for defense, such as those seen in autism as meltdowns and tantrums, which compromises higher brain structures related to learning and sociality. From this perspective, an autonomic nervous system in a state of defense leads to hypersensitivities and tantrums while compromising sociality, state regulation, social communication, auditory processing, speech, and cognitive function. Implicit in this perspective is the possibility of the individual changing state, becoming calmer and spontaneously social, when signals of threat are reduced and signals of safety are increased (see Porges, 2022).

Studies that apply Polyvagal Theory's conceptualization of autonomic reactivity to the psychological construct of autism have documented low ventral vagal influences on the heart measured via respiratory sinus arrhythmia (Bal et al., 2010; Patriquin et al., 2013, 2019; Van Hecke et al., 2009). According to the Polyvagal Theory, reduction of this vagal circuit—the removal of the vagal brake—potentiates the other components of the autonomic nervous system (i.e., sympathetic nervous system, dorsal vagal pathways) that support defense. These autonomic pathways, consistent with features commonly observed in those diagnosed with autism, support symptoms of anxiety and defensiveness. This supports an autonomic substrate for behaviors often observed as either tantrums and meltdowns (via the sympathetic nervous system) or immobilizations, social withdrawal, and total behavioral shutdown (via dorsal vagal pathways).

Polyvagal Theory (Porges, 1998) expanded its potential utility for understanding underlying mechanisms in expressed features of autism by introducing a social engagement system that links neural regulation of the face and head with vagal pathways to the heart (i.e., vagal brake). In structuring this face-heart connection as a social engagement system and linking it to the ventral vagus, several symptoms of autism could now be explained, such as hypersensitivities, hyposensitivity to human voice, atypical vocal intonation, dampened facial expressivity, auditory processing deficits, language delay, and selective eating. These autonomic states of defense become efficiently available when the calming ventral vagal circuit (vagal brake) is withdrawn. Polyvagal Theory identified the functioning of the vagal brake via measures of respiratory sinus arrhythmia (i.e., a respiratory pattern in the beat-to-beat heart rate pattern) as a physiological index that could be monitored to infer accessibility to the social engagement system that would promote physiological calmness and sociality. In the absence of a resilient vagal brake (i.e., poor vagal efficiency), the autonomic state could promote the primitive survival strategies frequently observed in autism. In addition to these obvious behavioral consequences, a loss of accessibility to the vagal brake (i.e., poor vagal efficiency) is also associated with a challenged digestive system locked in a pervasive defensiveness, with such symptoms as nausea, diarrhea, constipation, and general gut pain frequently associated with autism (Kolacz et al., 2019; 2022b).

Polyvagal Theory uses the process of neuroception to describe neural mechanisms that reflexively detect safety or threat and reflexively shift autonomic state to promote adaptive behaviors. Although virtually all living organisms detect signals of threat, mammals seem to have a unique form of neuroception that enables them to downregulate threat reactions through signals of safety. The classic example is the prosodic voice (range of intonation) of a mother in calming her infant. In fact, we have conducted research documenting that greater maternal vocal prosody is more effective in calming infants following a stressor (Kolacz et al., 2022a). Consistent with Polyvagal Theory, understanding parameters of acoustic signals of safety have led to an innovative intervention that uses acoustic stimulation, similar to a mother's lullaby, to move an infant from tantrum to calm. The intervention, known as the Safe and Sound Protocol (Heilman et al., 2023; Porges et al., 2013; 2014), has successfully been applied to autistic individuals with documented effects of calming, reducing hypersensitivities, improving auditory processing, and enhancing ventral vagal regulation of the heart.

Consistent with the title of this book, when autism is viewed through the lens of the Polyvagal Theory, several features associated with a diagnosis of autism can be explained as naturally occurring biobehavioral phenomena associated with an autonomic state of defense, without being determined by genes, requiring a diagnosis, or being irreversibly permanent. Thus, many features associated with the diagnosis can be observed in neurotypical individuals when they are in states of chronic threat. This model can even explain other autonomic issues frequently associated with an autism diagnosis, such as gut problems and inflammatory diseases. In addition, Polyvagal Theory provides insights into new intervention models, including a deeper understanding of the inherent neural mechanisms that may be recruited to mitigate threat reaction. This has led to an emphasis on a neurophysiology of safety (Porges, 2022) that explains how signals of safety recruit the ventral vagus and promote calm autonomic states that support homeostatic functions (health, growth, restoration) and sociality.

Polyvagal Theory assumes that the autonomic nervous system provides the neural platform upon which different clusters of behaviors may spontaneously emerge. When the autonomic nervous system has access to the ventral vagal complex, the social engagement system is available to dynamically interact and co-regulate with others. This form of sociality involves signals of safety and social communication through facial expressions and vocal intonation. Functionally, when the nervous system detects safety, the ventral vagal circuit is preeminent, enabling the vagal brake to dynamically and efficiently regulate autonomic state to calm, support homeostatic functions, and promote sociality. However, if the nervous system detects threat, the vagal brake becomes unavailable. Under these conditions, the autonomic nervous system shifts from a state that is calm and social to defensive states that support either fight-flight behaviors or withdrawal and shutdown. Thus, Polyvagal Theory emphasizes that many of the features that we assume are lifelong characteristics of autism may instead be the product of a nervous system in a chronic state of threat. About 20 years ago several of these features were introduced to the autism research community (Porges, 2005) during a period of expanding interests in the neurobiology of autism (see Bauman & Kemper, 2005). However, at that time funding initiatives heavily focused on genetic and imaging technologies and did not prioritize research on the autonomic nervous system as a powerful intervening variable mediating diagnostic symptoms.

Since research focusing on genetic and cortical mapping has had limited impact on the welfare of individuals with autism, we now have an opportunity to support initiatives that focus on the role autonomic state plays in the expression of symptoms. *Autism in Polyvagal Terms: New Possibilities and Interventions* is consistent with this perspective. Optimistically, research is beginning to document that interventions can be designed as neural exercises that have profound effects on social behavior and hypersensitivities, by reengaging the vagal brake and enabling the social engagement system to become more accessible (e.g., Heilman et al., 2023; Porges et al., 2013; 2014).

—Stephen W. Porges, PhD

WORKS CITED

Bal, E., Harden, E., Lamb, D., Van Hecke, A. V., Denver, J. W., & Porges, S. W. (2010). Emotion recognition in children with autism spectrum disorders: Relations to eye gaze and autonomic state. *Journal of Autism and Developmental Disorders, 40*, 358–370.

Bauman, M. L., & Kemper, T. L. (Eds.). (2005). *The neurobiology of autism.* Johns Hopkins University Press.

Heilman, K. J., Heinrich, S., Achermann, M., Nix, E., & Kyuchukov, H. (2023). Effects of the Safe and Sound Protocol (SSP) on sensory processing, digestive function and selective eating in children and adults with autism: A prospective single-arm study. *Journal on Developmental Disabilities, 20*(1). https://oadd.org/wp-content/uploads/2023/04/V28-N1-JoDD-21-388R-Heilman-et-al-v2.pdf

Kolacz, J., daSilva, E. B., Lewis, G. F., Bertenthal, B. I., & Porges, S. W. (2022a). Associations between acoustic features of maternal speech and infants' emotion regulation following a social stressor. *Infancy, 27*(1), 135–158.

Kolacz, J., Kovacic, K., Dang, L., Li, B. U., Lewis, G. F., & Porges, S. W. (2022b). Cardiac vagal regulation is impeded in children with cyclic vomiting syndrome. *American Journal of Gastroenterology, 118*(7), 1268–1275. https://doi.org/10.14309/ajg.0000000000002207

Kolacz, J., Kovacic, K. K., & Porges, S. W. (2019). Traumatic stress and the autonomic brain-gut connection in development: Polyvagal Theory as an integrative framework for psychosocial and gastrointestinal pathology. *Developmental Psychobiology, 61*(5), 796–809.

Lord, C., Rutter, M., DiLavore, P., & Risi, S. (1999). Autism Diagnostic Observation Schedule (ADOS). Western Psychological Services.

Lord, C., Storoschuk, S., Rutter, M., & Pickles, A. (1993). Using the ADI-R to diagnose autism in preschool children. *Infant Mental Health Journal, 14(3)*, 234–252.

Patriquin, M. A., Scarpa, A., Friedman, B. H., & Porges, S. W. (2013). Respiratory sinus arrhythmia: A marker for positive social functioning and receptive language skills in children with autism spectrum disorders. *Developmental Psychobiology, 55*(2), 101–112.

Porges, S. W. (1976). Peripheral and neurochemical parallels of psychopathology: A psychophysiological model relating autonomic imbalance to hyperactivity, psychopathy, and autism. *Advances in Child Development and Behavior, 11*, 35–65.

Porges, S. W. (1995). Orienting in a defensive world: Mammalian modifications of our evolutionary heritage. A Polyvagal Theory. *Psychophysiology, 32*(4), 301–318.

Porges, S. W. (1998). Love: An emergent property of the mammalian autonomic nervous system. *Psychoneuroendocrinology, 23*(8), 837–861.

Porges, S. W. (2005). The vagus: A mediator of behavioral and physiologic features associated with autism. In M. L. Bauman & T. L. Kemper (Eds.), *The neurobiology of autism* (pp. 65–78). Johns Hopkins University Press.

Porges, S. W. (2022). Polyvagal Theory: A science of safety. *Frontiers in Integrative Neuroscience, 16*, 27.

Porges, S. W., Bazhenova, O. V., Bal, E., Carlson, N., Sorokin, Y., Heilman, K. J., Cook, E. H., & Lewis, G. F. (2014). Reducing auditory hypersensitivities in autistic spectrum disorder: Preliminary findings evaluating the listening project protocol. *Frontiers in Pediatrics, 2*, 80.

Porges, S. W., Macellaio, M., Stanfill, S. D., McCue, K., Lewis, G. F., Harden, E. R., Handelman, M., Denver, J., Bazhenova, O. V. & Heilman, K. J. (2013). Respiratory sinus arrhythmia and auditory processing in autism: Modifiable deficits of an integrated social engagement system? *International Journal of Psychophysiology, 88*(3), 261–270.

Van Hecke, A. V., Lebow, J., Bal, E., Lamb, D., Harden, E., Kramer, A., Denver, J., Bazhenova, O., & Porges, S. W. (2009). Electroencephalogram and heart rate regulation to familiar and unfamiliar people in children with autism spectrum disorders. *Child Development, 80*(4), 1118–1133.

Autism in Polyvagal Terms

Why Autism and Polyvagal Theory?

It's always a risk to take action. It might not work, it might blow up in your face, you might lose money, you might fail. No one may get it.

But that's not the only risk. There's another risk: the risk of not trying it . . . of continuing in the same direction in the same way, wondering about other paths and possibilities, believing that this is as good as it gets while discontent gnaws away at your soul.

ROB BELL, *HOW TO BE HERE*

My experience with autism started at 18 and has carried with me to now. It regularly makes social interaction challenging, and at times it has led to its own forms of discrimination in important moments in my life. On the flipside, having a restrictive and repetitive interest in certain topics—a characteristic trait of autism—has led to a long journey of discovery of the self. During that journey, I have come to understand autism as a *disordering of the evolutionary journey of my own nervous system*.

In my clinical practice with both children and adults, I have noticed a great degree of overlap in symptoms when diagnosing autism, posttraumatic stress disorder, and obsessive-compulsive disorder. These similarities have given me pause on a number of occasions, and they began to turn me toward the work of Dr. Stephen Porges on Polyvagal Theory. I had first encountered this work in my clinical training, during a workshop related to Sensorimotor Psychotherapy a body-based psychotherapy for the treatment of trauma. Since popularized by the work of such writers as Gabor Maté, Pat Ogden, Bessel Van der Kolk, and Deb Dana, Polyvagal Theory has emerged in the last decade as a hallmark of how to understand trauma in the context of the human body. Dr. Porges has become a mentor of sorts and guided me into projects with the Kinsey Institute, where I deepened my scholastic understanding of autism from a polyvagal perspective.

A FEW BROAD DEFINITIONS

Before going further, let's briefly discuss some terms that recur throughout this book. This overview introduces these terms and describes the chapters that unpacked these concepts. More detailed definitions of the key terms and others highlighted throughout this book can be found in the glossary at the back.

POLYVAGAL THEORY is a framework for understanding how humans have evolved to respond to safety and threat. In the age of asocial reptiles, the most ancient part of the nervous system, the DORSAL VAGAL SYSTEM, emerged. This system is responsible for the collapse or shutdown response under stress, similar to a turtle hiding in its shell. Then, along came the SYMPATHETIC NERVOUS SYSTEM. Responsible for what is popularly known as the fight-or-flight response, this system enabled our mammalian ancestors to fend off predators: think of an elephant using its tusks to fend off a lion. It also enabled them to flee in the face of threat: think of a gazelle attempting to outrun a lion. Finally, a social engagement system began to emerge in primitive mammals. This change was dependent on an innovation in the regulation of our AUTONOMIC NERVOUS SYSTEM called the VENTRAL VAGAL SYSTEM, which allowed our mammalian ancestors to band together for survival. In the 200 million years since, this change and the way it has evolved in mammals have allowed humans to move from a more isolated hunter-gatherer lifestyle on the savannah to the modern, postindustrialized, communal existence we know today.

AUTISM, like POSTTRAUMATIC STRESS DISORDER and OBSESSIVE–COMPULSIVE DISORDER, can be understood as a disordering of how much time the human nervous system spends in the sympathetic nervous (FIGHT-OR-FLIGHT) system and dorsal vagal (COLLAPSE-OR-FREEZE) system. Cardiac studies repeatedly demonstrate that people with autism have higher heart rates and, as a result, a lower VAGAL TONE: a measure of how well the vagus nerve is functioning, measured through the respiratory pattern (i.e., respiratory sinus arrhythmia) embedded in beat-to-beat HEART RATE VARIABILITY (HRV). In general, heart rate tracks vagal tone. That is, reduced vagal influence is observed as the time between heart beats becomes shorter, and increased vagal influence is observed as the time between beats becomes longer (Ruscio, 2022). As a general rule, the faster one's heart rate and the lower the HRV, the more likely the individual is in an autonomic state characterized by sympathetic or dorsal vagal activation. In other words, a person with autism lives in an autonomic state that is likely to provoke threat reactions like fight-or-flight or shutdown.

As I have come to understand myself and my own cardiac health through this lens, and adopt a polyvagal perspective on my existence, I have become increasingly aware that my autism has modulated over time. When I was 18 and facing some legal challenges, I was more rigid and more inflexible and had worse social skills than I do now, when I am overemployed and supported by good stress-management skills. Thus, I have displayed more or fewer autistic traits, in terms of core symptoms, at different points in my life course, depending on how much of a sense of safety I could access through the ventral vagal system.

NEUROCEPTION is a term coined by Dr. Porges to describe a key concept within this framework: the less-than-conscious process by which we as humans detect a sense of safety or threat. And while we might like to believe that all nervous systems function identically, they do not—some are less inclined to reside in states of threat than others. Within the field of psychotherapy this has been witnessed in those with trauma histories; historically the work has often been to help clients begin to recognize when they are having flashbacks and to learn to change their responses to these moments of dysregulation or lack of homeostasis. The nervous system of autistic individuals is generally considered to be atypical in presentation, compared to their nonautistic peers, though this finding is contested by some (see Chapter 1). We might see people with autism more often than those without in states of fight/flight or collapse, particularly in public spaces: the child screaming in the airport, the student running from a special education teacher, and the teen who freezes when asked a question in class are common, relatable examples for most people who hear the phrase "autistic behaviors."

This stereotype illustrates how easily the human mind associates autism with aggressive, evasive, and collapse-type behaviors. But why? Historically, answers to this question have invoked the concepts of neurodiversity and/or neuroplasticity. The term NEURODIVERSITY, originally identified by Judy Singer in 1999, describes an unidentified neuroanatomical or neurochemical difference that leads to differences in thought processes and behaviors—differences that others might consider socially unacceptable. NEUROPLASTICITY refers to the ability of neural networks in the brain to reorient themselves to promote growth and potentially take on new functions. As a result of these neural axons firing in new directions, the brain is considered to have the ability to rewire itself for new tasks (Costandi, 2016). Akin to its cousin "neurodiversity," "neuroplasticity" reflects the underlying premise that these differences in neural wiring are what results in differences in behavior and/or thought processes, and that this wiring can be changed.

From a polyvagal perspective, however, we depart from this notion of differential wiring in favor of state changes. Consider a light switch on the wall: when the switch is flipped one way the light turns on and illuminates the room, and when the switch is turned the other way the room is dark. The light we want to turn on for individuals with autism is a state change to a feeling of safety. The neural exercises I propose in this book as a treatment for autism involve intentionally *flipping the vagal switch*, repeatedly, so that individuals with autism can increasingly occupy states of safety by flipping the switch themselves. By a vagal switch, what is meant in this text is the idea of taking the autistic autonomic nervous system from a position of chronic threat through interventions, into a state of safety. This state of safety, while only temporary, can be strengthened over time, like a muscle, in autistic autonomic nervous systems. The immediate result (depending on the intervention) is either increased social engagement or decreased cognitive inflexibility, and the longer-term effect as the muscle builds results in being more socially connected and more cognitively flexible. This concept of a light switch is one that will be used throughout to illustrate the concept of vagal efficiency.

For individuals with autism the desired state of feeling safe—all too unfamiliar to them—is achievable only if we flip the switch enough times for them to learn to flip the switch themselves. If we give autistic individuals the right set of tools and experiences in a therapeutic space (see Chapters 6, 7, 9, and 10), we can begin to create a state shift. And through these state shifts, our autistic patients can begin to experience life in a less evasive, aggressive, and collapsed way. In short, they can begin to increasingly experience the light of connection with their fellow human beings.

NEURAL EXERCISES, the subject of this book, are a clinical therapy model that defines autism in terms of lack of COGNITIVE FLEXIBILITY and connects difficulty with social skills to lower vagal tone. It addresses these core problems for the purpose of flipping the vagal switch, through such strategies as biofeedback, motivational interviewing, mindfulness, and exercise, as well as social work/clinical psychology pedagogy and establishing a sense of safety between client and therapist. The goal of this set of approaches is to reduce cognitive rigidity and improve social connectedness by helping our clients modulate vagal tone. Many of the interventions and exercises described in Parts 2 and 3 of this book can easily be fused with existing modes of therapy, such as Sensorimotor Psychotherapy (Ogden et al., 2006; Ogden & Fisher, 2015) and cognitive behavioral therapy.

This work is not entirely my own—I ground it in values that have been shown to work in such historical modalities as Sensorimotor Psychotherapy (Ogden et al., 2006) and motivational interviewing. The neural exercises in this book are inspired by and embody the term "viscera" in "*viscero*motor," collectively referring to the internal organs, especially the heart, liver, and stomach. These somatic psychotherapy roots have sprouted visceromotor solutions that build on this notion that body-based changes translate into meaningful internal changes in the visceral system. When we dig into the work of Pat Ogden and Bill Miller, we find values like organicity and collaboration that are very similar to those espoused here. I hope you, too, will evince these values as you work and live with or on the spectrum.

WHAT THIS BOOK IS AND IS NOT

This book is intended as a starting point, rather than an all-inclusive guide, to working with clients with autism from a polyvagal perspective. Although autism is one of the better researched diagnoses affecting humanity, we still have a very limited pool of information on how to help people with autism modulate their core symptoms, especially since many insurance companies will reimburse only for autism treatments using APPLIED BEHAVIORAL ANALYSIS (ABA). Although it can be a useful tool, like other therapeutic modalities ABA has been limited in its accomplishments.

These chapters present a series of alternative, VISCEROMOTOR PSYCHOTHERAPY tools to consider. Each of these specific strategies shared a central purpose of developing a strong therapeutic alliance—we know from lots of research that the alliance between therapist and client matters more than modality. Thus, the strategies in this book have been developed with an eye toward forming strong relationships with clients who have challenges relating to others. The values that underlie these strategies are as follows:

1. KINDNESS: Responding in the gentlest and easiest way we can, achieved by being attuned to our own autonomic nervous system and the autonomic nervous system of others

2. QUALITY: Excellence, reliability, ethics, integrity, professionalism, responsiveness to emerging evidence (MINT, n.d.)

3. OPENNESS: Evolving, emergent, open-minded, innovative, flexible, expanding the boundaries, growth, humility, curiosity, self-critical (MINT, n.d.)

4. GENEROSITY: Nonpossessiveness, sharing, acknowledgment, collaboration, cooperation, giving more than you receive (MINT, n.d.)

5. RESPECT: Valuing individual and professional diversity; demonstrating internationality, kindness, listening, communication, egalitarianism (MINT, n.d.)

6. ORGANICITY: The internal wisdom of all living systems; the healing power and intelligence that is within; our own unique, mysterious, and emergent growth path within each of us that the therapist nurtures (Sensorimotor Psychotherapy Institute, 2022)

7. MINDFULNESS: Encouraging present-moment awareness of both client and therapist experiences, to call attention to this present-moment awareness (a principle likely useful only if it is as self-directed and concerned with transference, as it is other-directed)

The integration of these values into treatment relies on therapists' willingness to go on their own journey of self-discovery. Values like generosity have a way of working on us, reshaping how we perceive ourselves. While it might be comfortable to think that as trained therapists we know quite a lot, the reality is often that there is much we have to learn about ourselves and our own limitations. These values have a way of working on us if we let them, revealing where our own growth edges are. One could easily spend several volumes exploring these values, but for the purposes of this book they serve as ethical guideposts both for serving our clients as therapists and for trying to be better human beings.

In keeping with these values, we view autism as a modifiable set of traits that ranges in severity and presentation. Terms like "low" and "high" functioning are widely held to be offensive, somewhat akin to the "r" word of the 1980s to refer clinically to slowness. It would not be consistent with this value system to say that one "outgrows" their autism, and it would not be kind or open-minded to do so. A more generous view is that there are more and less optimal ways to function with what we now know as autism spectrum disorder.

My hope is that this book helps therapists help persons with ASD achieve their optimal level of functioning within their specific constellation of symptoms. A polyvagal perspective sees these symptoms as transient and changeable, and it is the task of the therapist to help the person with autism work on their own goals related to reducing cognitive inflexibility and/or improving interpersonal social communication skills. Thus, it is with optimism that I share these visceromotor psychotherapy tools. I hope this will be a game-changer for your patients with autism spectrum disorder. In the spirit of the quote from Rob Bell at the top of this introduction, the risk of *not* trying a new approach—of "believing that this is as good as it gets"—may be greater than taking the leap to try something new.

I feel the need to share that some of the content in this book is intense and, perhaps, at moments, difficult to swallow. Even the word "trauma," the way it's said through the roll of the "t" and the "r," suggests a degree of roughness. This book is not for the fainthearted. Clinical work that involves trauma is not easy to do, or to read about. I note this ahead of time in case you have your own history that may intersect with some of the narratives in these chapters.

Please note also that the case studies I describe are derived from actual cases in my practice, but they are nonetheless composites—they do not represent transcripts of actual sessions, and I use fictitious names. They nonetheless exemplify approaches and dialogue I have found effective in my practice.

PART 1

Autism, Neurobiology, and the Nervous System

CHAPTER 1

The Autonomic Nervous System

··

The complexity of diagnosing someone with autism is immense. Texture or light sensitivity, difficulty with eye contact, challenges talking about emotions, fear of social interactions—all these are symptoms of both AUTISM SPECTRUM DISORDER (ASD) and POSTTRAUMATIC STRESS DISORDER (PTSD). Across the autistic life course, trauma and autism are strongly linked. This connection leads us to Polyvagal Theory.

Polyvagal Theory, as noted in the Introduction, refers to how the human autonomic nervous system (Figure 1.1) has evolved over millions of years and is hierarchically organized into three distinct parts, each responsible for a different set of responses to stress or threat. As Stephen Porges (1994) writes, "The Polyvagal Theory proposes that the evolution of the mammalian autonomic nervous system provides the neurophysiological substrates for adaptive behavioral strategies" (see also Porges 1995, 2009; Porges et al., 1996; Sargunaraj et al., 1996). The DORSAL VAGAL SYSTEM is the most ancient of the parts. It is responsible for freeze and collapse responses, which may look like rigidity of thought, depression, numbness, a raised pain threshold, hopelessness, and ultimately complete shutdown. The sympathetic nervous system is responsible for fight-or-flight responses, which may be expressed as lack of eye contact, difficulty with social communication, anger, rage, irritation, anxiety, running, tantrums, or even fighting. The third part, the ventral vagal system, is often termed the "social engagement system"

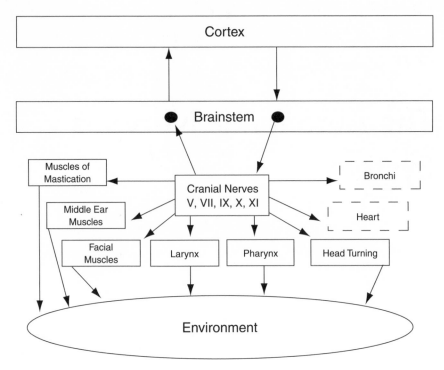

Figure 1.1: Autonomic nervous system
Source: The Vagal Paradox: A polyvagal solution by Stephen W. Porges, www.sciencedirect
.com/journal/comprehensive-psychoneuroendocrinology, licensed under CC BY 4.0 https://
creativecommons.org/licenses/by/4.0/.

and is responsible for calm, socially connected actions and communication. It
is from this grounded place that we experience a deep sense of safety via the
mechanism of *neuro*ception, a less conscious, more subjective experience than
our direct *per*ception of the world. As Porges (2017) so eloquently defines it,
"Neuroception evaluates risk in the environment without awareness. Perception implies awareness and conscious detection. Neuroception is not a cognitive
process; it is a neural process without a dependency on awareness." Thus, NEU-
ROCEPTION is an essential process to engage with our fellow humans in shared
feelings of safety. In terms of an evolutionary adaptation, this process of shared
safety allowed our ancestors to work together and, ultimately, to emerge from
the savannah and form agrarian societies, leading to the present world as we
know it. From a therapeutic perspective, the ventral vagal state provides a place

from which to understand clients' defensive actions as well intended, rather than unhelpful expressions of who they are.

Thus, Polyvagal Theory provides both a neuroanatomical framework to explore our expressions of behavior and thought, and a way to understand people that goes beyond general medical or even mental health diagnosis. To illustrate, let's look at stories about different types of nervous system responses, about different expressions of the cranial nerve, and discuss how we can understand autism through this lens of states of threat.

REST: THE VENTRAL VAGAL STATE

Perhaps the best day of every parent's life is when their first child is born. Imagine a boy about seven pounds with big brown eyes and the tiniest little fingers. As the father stares in awe and amazement, the boy's crying ceases and he nuzzles in close. Perhaps it's the pheromones, or the familiar sound of the father's voice, but it is as if the boy just ceased being nervous. It is this shared sense of safety or peace that gives humans the most wonderful moments of shared gaze, laughter, and joy.

Everything about this picture gives an onlooker an image of safety: the gaze of the father and the child, the cessation of the crying, and the familiar sense of recognition that passes between the man and the boy. We know from research on maternal vocalizations that following a stressor the familiar maternal prosody is sufficient to calm an infant (Kolacz et al., 2022). This provides not only a window into how safety is experienced but also a clue as to what the nonautistic experience is like. Safety is this elusive feeling that for many autistic persons is a rare or even completely foreign experience. With autistic clients, the work of psychotherapy is to cultivate this elusive experience within the therapy space.

FIGHT: THE SYMPATHETIC STATE

Fight, a response of the sympathetic branch of the autonomic nervous system, is an experience chiseled deep in the human consciousness. For individuals with autism, not only is the fight response deeply engrained, but it is also arguably a cardiac norm. Studies have consistently found that the cardiac profiles of children with autism differ from those of their nonautistic peers (Owens et al., 2021; Parma et al., 2021; Patriquin et al., 2019; Porges, 2005; Porges et al., 2013, 2014). This well-established correlation between the presence of autism and increased levels of cardiac output suggests that autism might be a disorder of altered auto-nomic regulation. In effect, the autistic person lives in a constant state of threat.

Consider an autistic client who from childhood experienced repeated alien-ation from his father. Alienation, as the word suggests, is a sense of feeling foreign to someone who should feel close and familiar. This client was the son of a pastor and his wife, who had her own mental health issues. His father was incredibly money driven and worked about 70 hours per week, likely as a result of his own traumas that refused to allow his nervous system to rest. When he came home, he would often take out his frustrations on both his wife and son, who was naturally curious. The boy would approach his dad about something, and his dad would generally shout at him. Occasionally, his father would also pick him up by the shoulders and throw his 50 pounds across the room, his torso crashing into the wall. The tears and whimpering that resulted were met with further shouting.

This example highlights an autonomic nervous system state in sharp contrast to the earlier, ventral vagal state of rest. It demonstrates how activation of the sympathetic nervous system can provoke a fight response. It should come as no surprise to clinicians that autistic clients are aggressive, given how much time they spend in a sympathetic state. Psychotherapy is about creating a safe space for clients, and for the autistic client it is about flipping the vagal switch that allows them to experience that rare and elusive feeling of safety.

FLIGHT: THE SYMPATHETIC STATE

Another potential response to the sympathetic state is flight. For instance, an autistic client told me that when he turned 18 he was reckless, short-sighted, and incapable of slowing down. He recounted that one day, driving to school, he was driving too fast, swerved into the other lane, and crashed into another vehi-cle. When this happened, his thinking went out the window, worry took over, and his ancient animal response to run kicked in. After leaving the scene of the accident, the boy spent the better part of an hour struggling before ultimately turning himself in to the police and being charged with hit and run.

This example highlights a flight response, a survival strategy that our mam-malian ancestors depended on. It was very useful, on the savannah, for priming the body to run, to escape a predator, but much less adaptive for an 18-year-old in modern day—flight was the opposite of helpful. His nervous system, hijacked by an increased level of threat, did what it was programmed to do: become more rigid and less flexible and focus exclusively on the moment.

Functionally, at such a moment the *ventral vagal circuit shuts down* to optimize access to the sympathetic nervous system for defense. Unlike the sympathetic and dorsal vagal systems, the ventral vagus is directly linked to the cranial nerves that control facial and head-turning muscles, as well as muscles in the middle ear, heart, pharynx, larynx, and so on. These are all muscle groups responsible for engaging another human being socially at restful times. Thus, when the fight/flight system becomes activated and the ventral vagal circuit shuts down, any human is likely to struggle with eye contact, with reading any type of emotion, and with being mentally flexible. For those in a chronic state of threat, such as clients with autism, these are routine rather than extraordinary responses.

COLLAPSE: THE DORSAL STATE

The collapse or shutdown response is the oldest of the defensive responses. A client of mine gave a talk on autism and psychotherapy for an autism event. A fact unknown to the audience was that she and her former fiancée had recently separated. She described experiencing a sense of numbness as she gave the talk, during which she was operating from instinct but unable to read her own feeling states (alexithymia) or to make eye contact.

A strategy that many people with autism excel at is the ability to camouflage socially, more commonly known as MASKING. This enables individuals with autism to blend in socially with peers, often at the expense of their own preferences and deeply held values. For instance, an individual may struggle with loud noises but suppress this to go on a date with a peer at a crowded restaurant, muting those preferences at their own expense. My client's masking during the talk at the autism event involved projecting confidence and appearing capable and dynamic to an audience of 1,600 people. All the while, however, her mind and self weren't fully present. This is the strength, and the challenge, of these adaptations: they are designed to help us survive, even if survival means disengaging from higher-order processes like emotional awareness.

My client was so socially disconnected (more autistic, perhaps) in that moment because she was experiencing the loss of the love of her life. Her nervous system was in a state of collapse. Thus, her report of being increasingly rigid, disconnected from her mind and body (or ability to read feelings), and out of conscious control of her facial expressions should come as no surprise. Even though her response to this heightened state of threat may have been hard for her audience to notice, it is likely one of her more characteristic autistic states. Facing a sudden massive change like the loss of a loved one (a commonly cited trauma symptom) is an experience that feels to the body like one is going to die, and it can activate collapse. In her case, this trauma brought up ancient and adaptive processes, which included loss of conscious awareness and key executive function skills like sense of time and self-regulation.

FIGHT/FLIGHT/COLLAPSE AND THE CONNECTION TO AUTISM

The symptoms of autism spectrum disorder (ASD), as listed by the ADOS-2 (Autism Diagnostic Observation Schedule, 2nd ed.), fall into three categories: social interaction deficits; difficulties with the "social aspects" of communication; and restrictive, repetitive, and stereotyped patterns of behavior, interests, and/or activities (Lord et al., 1999). This is perhaps the best working definition of autism I have encountered, and there is wide agreement among psychologists about what autism is. However, autism has a variety of expressions—why the word "spectrum" is used to describe them.

The *Diagnostic and Statistical Manual of Mental Disorders* (*DSM*), fourth edition (text revision) (*DSM-4-TR*), had four separate diagnoses for this range of symptoms; the *DSM-5* combined these into one diagnosis (autism), which was updated (with a qualifier) in the *DSM-5-TR*. This is how we can have examples of autism ranging from the highly successful Elon Musk to the serial killer Jeffrey Dahmer (rumored to have been autistic but never clinically diagnosed).

A POLYVAGAL THEORY–INFORMED MODEL OF AUTISM SPECTRUM DISORDER

In this book, I take a polyvagal approach to understanding ASD and to outlining the clinical practices that help clients with autism reach states of safety. Most of the evidence showing that the expression of autistic symptoms is exacerbated by a state-specific condition is found in studies of HRV (Owens et al., 2021; Parma et al., 2021; Patriquin et al., 2011, 2019; Porges, 2005; Porges et al., 2013). Thus, rather than pursuing explanations of ASD based on behavioral symptoms, we will think of it as rooted in the functioning of the human heart.

RESTING HEART RATE refers to the number of heart beats per minute. A commonly used tool in medicine, it measures a variety of health-related factors. Broadly stated, the faster the heart is beating, the shorter the duration between the beats. If someone has a higher resting heart rate and lower HEART RATE VARIABILITY (HRV), they are more likely to be in a state of fight/flight or freeze and more likely to appear autistic. Conversely, those whose hearts take fewer beats per minute and have higher HRV are less likely to be in a state of fight/flight or freeze and are in turn less likely to look autistic. Thus, autism might be thought of as a state-specific condition, as being in a chronic state of fight, flight, or freeze that activates both the sympathetic and dorsal vagal systems.

This polyvagal perspective, which associates autism with trauma, is not meant to reopen the long-closed "refrigerator parent" debate over whether or not parental neglect (a form of trauma) is the cause of autism. Following a highly publicized 1949 paper in which Leo Kanner described "parental coldness, obsessiveness, and a mechanical type of attention to material needs only" as a hypothetical cause of autism, when a child was diagnosed with autism children's services would become involved, taking kids away from their homes. In no way is this book intended to resurrect this debunked theory or the practices that it encouraged.

From a Polyvagal Theory–informed perspective, for instance, in my client who was thrown against walls by his father, trauma had activated a chronic state of threat, yet that childhood experience may not be the sole reason for his high heart rate and low HRV. His frequent rigidity and difficulty with social interactions could have any number of causes. Explanations like genetic factors, environment, and how sensory information is processed by any of the seven senses (five senses plus interoception and proprioception) all are plausible explanations for his autistic behaviors. And in any case, the parental abuse my client suffered as a child is of a different order entirely than the emotional neglect Kanner hypothesized had left children "neatly in refrigerators which did not defrost." In short, while we can't assume trauma is the root cause of autism, with all the dangerous implications this assumption brings, we can say it could be one contributing cause among many others, genetic, sensory related, or otherwise.

The brief summary that follows illustrates how the three main categories of symptoms from the ADOS-2 definition of autism are related to research on HRV:

1. *Deficits in social interaction:* In polyvagal terms, this involves decreased social engagement during activation of the sympathetic nervous system (fight/flight or freeze). People with lower HRV struggle with
   — Empathy expression (Lischke et al., 2018)
   — Facial expression control (Porges, 2005; Porges et al., 2013, 2014)
   — ALEXITHYMIA: difficulty describing and labeling one's emotional experience, and an external orientation of thinking (Kinnaird et al., 2019; Lischke et al., 2018)

2. *Difficulties with the "social aspects" of communication:*
   — People with lower HRV struggle to maintain eye contact, and people with autism also struggle with eye contact (Porges, 2005; Porges et al., 2013, 2014).
   — People with higher HRV tend to demonstrate better social skills, joint attention, and language abilities (Patriquin et al., 2019).

3. *Restrictive, repetitive, and stereotyped patterns of behavior, interests, and/or activities:*
   — HRV is significantly correlated with performance on tasks involving cognitive flexibility (Alba et al., 2019).
   — Higher resting heart rate suggests greater cognitive flexibility that is state specific (Alba et al., 2019; Colzato et al., 2018).

A PERSONAL NARRATIVE TO UNPACK A POLYVAGAL MODEL OF AUTISM

A more personal way of understanding the connection between autism and Polyvagal Theory is to share an episode from my own life, from January to April of 2019, when I met and began a relationship with Stella. She brought some semblance of order to my world. In January 2019 I was a social worker at a nursing home, feeling aimless and begrudging toward my own life. I felt stuck in northern Wisconsin, for the sake of my boys, one of whom might have described me as rather rigid. My schedule depended on me leaving work at 5 p.m., in order to get home from my hour-long commute in time to pick up my boys; if clients had needs at the very end of the day, they would wait until the next day because I had to leave, and my time was precious. However, from my employer's perspective I was liable for all those needs, even the ones that went well past 5 p.m. I was salaried, which to my boss meant that I would do social work whenever he needed it. In his eyes, I was largely inflexible, while from my perspective I was supporting my family by maintaining boundaries. And to be successful in this role would have meant taking his criticisms seriously, which I did not. As a by-product of this rigidity, my work relationships suffered, with my boss, the office manager, and the director of nursing. And so my time there became increasingly unpleasant, and I became more and more withdrawn.

And then came Stella, in early January. We connected instantly; it was as if I had known her all along, and the world made sense. As we dated, I increasingly began to recognize the difference in my own understanding of my role and that of my supervisors. When I acknowledged this, my relationships with others improved as I tried to be more able to meet my boss's needs. However, given the difference in priorities between my supervisor and myself, in March 2019 I decided to leave the position, with no idea where I was going—call it a leap of faith. The safety and security of the relationship with Stella gave me the courage to begin not only to set my boundaries but also to hold to them firmly as I explored new directions, like psychotherapy with children and adults. And this ability to shift and move was all because of a state of feeling safe enough in a dating relationship to take a risk. One might say the vagal switch was turned on through the experience of safe and heartfelt connection, and the experience of safety allowed me to shift, to move into a more ventral vagal state.

If for those four months someone had been monitoring my heart rate, I expect it would have shown a progressive increase, along with a decrease in HRV, followed by a slowing of heart rate and an increase in HRV as I experienced signals of safety from Stella and changed my work environment. It is similar for our autistic clients. The experience of feeling safe is not a sudden flood but, rather, a gradual introduction to a sense of safety. It comes from flipping the vagal switch on, again and again, which creates a familiarity with a state with more flexibility, openness, creativity, and connections to the multifaceted social world.

SHARED EXPERTISE

Power is a strong focus in this book. I often use the word EXPERTISE, which refers to who is responsible for decision making based on the primacy of knowledge. In the visceromotor psychotherapy model of treatment, expertise is something that is shared. Clinical expertise is valuable for understanding concepts such as a polyvagal model of autism and for using strategies like motivational interviewing and applied behavioral analysis. However, this kind of expertise does not extend to making decisions for others who live with autism, who have their own internal autistic wisdom. That lived wisdom must share equal weight with professional expertise, especially since in social environments this wisdom is often overlooked. This is not to say that all things an autistic person says we should agree to, but their expertise must be accepted within a secure therapeutic relationship to facilitate safety.

THE POLYVAGAL MODEL OF AUTISM VERSUS TRADITIONAL MODELS

A number of key differences distinguish a polyvagal model of autism from a traditional understanding of the disorder, differences that have significant implications for treatment. As Table 1.1 illustrates, traditional models of autism tend to rely on a theory of differential wiring and/or anatomy. This runs counter to how Polyvagal Theory conceptualizes a person on the autism spectrum, as someone whose autonomic nervous system is in a chronic state of threat. This difference in the Polyvagal Theory concept of the origins of autism leads to the conclusion that, over the life course, people with autism can show more or fewer autistic

Table 1.1: The Polyvagal Model of Autism Versus Traditional Models		
	Traditional Models of Autism	**Polyvagal-Informed Models of Autism**
Origin	Differential anatomy or wiring	Chronic states of fight/flight and collapse
Duration	Lifelong and enduring	Enduring but modifiable over the life course
Symptoms	Deficits in social communication and restrictive, repetitive patterns of interests or behaviors	Dampened social engagement system and mental inflexibility

Treatment outlook	Symptoms do not change	Symptoms change over time
Recommended treatment	Applied behavioral analysis, occupational and speech therapy	Safe and Sound Protocol, compassionate ABA, mindfulness, biofeedback, motivational interviewing, cognitive behavioral therapy, EMDR, Sensorimotor Psychotherapy speech and occupational therapy
Treatment goals	Compliance, reduction of maladaptive behaviors, activities of daily living (e.g., brushing teeth, potty training), development of language skills, sensory integration	Auditory integration, reducing difficult behaviors, establishing a sense of safety, increasing social communication, increasing mental flexibility, increasing coping skills, increasing body awareness, integration and organization of memories, communication skills, building vagal regulation, increasing motor skills, sensory integration, addressing maladaptive beliefs

traits: they can become less or more flexible and less or more socially connected to others. The polyvagal model assumes that autism can be modulated via time, intervention, and discovery. More traditional models assume that autism is lifelong and enduring; hence health insurance systems like Medicaid reimburse only for symptom modulation treatments, like applied behavioral analysis (ABA).

I should add that I understand some of you may be offended by the term "disorder" to describe autism, although this is how the *DSM-5-TR* refers to it. As I've said elsewhere, I believe it is an insult and an exercise of privilege to *not* call it a disorder. The many people I serve who are cognitively rigid or struggling with social connectedness see the way their neurobiology functions as a disorder. For these clients, to call their experience with this thing we call "autism" something other than a disorder would be highly off-putting. With respect to privilege, I think influencers on social media who opine that autism is not a disorder occupy a special space where there is little to no accountability for recommending society change to allow them to be themselves. In reality, many of my clients occupy societal spaces where such pie-in-the-sky type approaches could even be danger-ous. And while this may even sound a bit alarmist, being overly optimistic in a position of extreme influence endangers people who model their lives after what they see, when perhaps the contexts are intricately different.

CRITICISMS OF A POLYVAGAL THEORY–INFORMED MODEL OF AUTISM

A number of critics have said that Polyvagal Theory is misapplied to autism. One cluster of articles is highlighted in the meta-analysis by Barbier et al. (2022), which makes a largely mathematical argument that in most studies reporting on RESPIRATORY SINUS ARRHYTHMIA (RSA) in patients with autism, the data falls within what would be considered a normative HRV range. Barbier and his team conclude that Porges's findings are incomplete and thus would challenge the underlying assumption by Porges of the importance of the concept of state shifting in ASD. They conclude that most studies written on the RSA in autism confirm the prior findings of Porges only because they are biased and inclined to do so, rather than because the results support the theory.

Here I outline the arguments Barbier et al. (2022) make against a Polyvagal Theory–informed model of ASD, and responses to these arguments.

RSA can be affected by other factors like blood pressure (citing Grossman & Taylor, 2007). RSA is primarily a measure of vagal tone, and it is not clear in the literature whether it is affected by other factors. That stated, the cited article does not discuss what Barbier et al. propose. RSA represents the "functional" output of the ventral vagus on the heart. Other influential factors, rather than being con-founds, may in fact identify targets for intervention. Breathing strategies, often derived from yoga, help calm the autonomic nervous system. For example, the calming experienced during slow exhalation aligns with the ventral vagal influ-ence on the heart, which is optimized during exhalation. Moreover, Grossman and Taylor (2007) use a confounded index of RSA (see Lewis et al., 2012).

Perceived attractiveness of Polyvagal Theory to understand autism is why other studies repeatedly confirm findings. At least 34 known independent studies have been conducted, over 18 years, that confirm these findings. While it might appear attractive to confirm an existing theory, these studies do so with independent research teams, at different times and locations across the globe, and with varying funding sources. Occam's razor suggests the simple explanation: there truly is a strong correlation between autism and levels of HRV.

Average differences in RSA, while consistent across autistic populations, are the by-product of not measuring against a normed level of RSA. This explanation includes studies that appear selected to fit their arguments, rather than the entirety of the literature. Barbier et al. cite absence of data as the reason for omitting these papers, yet there is no mention that they reached out to the study authors to attain the data.

When placed against normative data, autistic RSA is in a normative range. There is no discussion of methodological differences in the studies, to determine which ones are and are not more accurate. For instance, as Porges (2021) writes so eloquently in his article "Polyvagal Theory: Background and Criticism":

> Research has documented (see Lewis et al., 2012) that the Grossman methodology is faulty in estimating ventral vagal tone and is directly the cause of their faulty inference regarding the inaccuracy of quantifying respiratory sinus arrhythmia as a valid index of ventral vagal tone. Research has documented (see Lewis et al., 2012) the precision and accuracy of the Porges-Bohrer methodology and contrasts it with the inadequate methods used by Grossman. The flaws in the Grossman method have been known and documented for about 25 years. (Byrne & Porges, 1996; Lewis et al., 2012)

The meta-analysis by Barbier et al. has little to no discussion of whether studies were included or weighted based on accuracy of measurement methodology. Thus, since the data set in question lacks inclusion criteria regarding accuracy of method, we can't assume conclusions drawn from it are accurate.

THE DIRECTION AND ORGANIZATION OF THIS BOOK

I have written this book as a therapist shaped by his own autistic experience, coming to the task with a love of research and a long-standing training in the pedagogy of social work and motivational interviewing. This work is near and dear to my heart. It is for people like me that I seek to fill this need, in the psychotherapy field, for both a neurobiological model of autism that has a basis in medical evidence, and a treatment model with enough flexibility to demonstrate change in symptomatology over time. It is not enough to propose a neurobiological model yet leave it to individual therapists, who often find working with this population intimidating, to unpack the model and translate it into clinical practice. I write this book for those seeking to help those like me, to give you a set of tools based on evidence and clinical expertise from a polyvagal perspective, to help expand how you think and serve people on the autism spectrum. It is my hope that this book helps shape a new model of evidence-based practice that helps autistic patients modulate their states over time (as much or as little as they may like).

In short, this book is for those who are interested in helping autistic folks improve their lives. Together we will explore how the problems of restrictive and repetitive patterns of thought and behavior can be adjusted through mindfulness, cardiovascular exercise, and motivational interviewing. We can learn to improve social deficits in communication for our clients by enhancing a sense of safety and through social work pedagogy to build change in symptomatology. As I note in the Introduction, these treatment strategies are guided by the values of kindness, quality, openness, generosity, respect, organicity, and mindfulness. It is my hope that, as we journey toward a more compassionate future, we can learn to change not only our clients' autonomic nervous systems but our own in the process.

Part 1 (Chapters 1–4) reviews the principles of the sympathetic nervous system and Polyvagal Theory, explores how it connects to autism, and discusses the values important for cultivating safety. Part 2 (Chapters 5–7) examines the nature of cognitive inflexibility and outlines some neural strategies for creating a state change that can help our clients be more cognitive flexible, by flipping the vagal switch. Part 3 (Chapters 8–10) then explores what social impairments look like and how neural strategies can create a state change that leads to increased social engagement. Parts 2 and 3 together provide a framework for incorporating a Polyvagal Theory–informed model of autism into existing psychotherapy models, such as motivational interviewing, cognitive behavioral therapy, and Sensorimotor Psychotherapy. Throughout, we consider how to apply these interventions in the context of autism-friendly values, based on the clinical and research heritage of psychologists Stephen Porges, Pat Ogden, Janina Fisher, Bill Miller, and Otto Rank. This work is indebted to the groundbreaking work of these predecessors.

CHAPTER 2

The Ventral Vagal System and Autism

....

The impulse to heal is real and powerful, and lies within the client. Our job is to evoke that healing power, to meet its tests and needs and to support it in its expression and development. We are not healers. We are the context in which healing is inspired.

RON KURTZ, *BODY-CENTERED PSYCHOTHERAPY* (2009),
AS CITED IN OGDEN (2021)

Imagine a mother and infant co-sleeping, with the infant's head resting on the mother's chest. Both the mother's and the son's eyes are closed and relaxed. Their nervous systems are co-regulating. The mother's, much larger, serves as a safety net for this tiny infant. It allows his back to relax, his eyes to close, and a sense of ease to move across his face. This is what we might more commonly refer to as a FELT SENSE OF SAFETY. The mother's much larger body and nervous system are providing his developing nervous system with familiar smells, body heat, a lower heart rate, a higher heart rate variability (HRV), and a physical enclosure whereby which he can let down his defenses. In this less than conscious process level of awareness defensive systems can come down, and they can both enter the ventral vagal system.

The above is not an atypical scene of mother and new baby. When the human threat detection system is not activated, our bodies are able, like those of this mother and son, to rest or socially engage. But the felt sense of safety depicted in this tableau is a bit of a rare thing in the autistic person's nervous system. As we begin to apply the polyvagal model to the constellation of symptoms we have come to know as autism spectrum disorder (ASD), notice what in their present moment prevents individuals with autism from feeling this sense of safety and connection.

THE VENTRAL VAGAL SYSTEM IN PEOPLE WITH AUTISM

Autism can be thought of as a chronic state of threat in which one consistently cannot achieve feelings of belonging. It is the task of therapists to try to cultivate this unfamiliar sense of safety illustrated by the mother and son. Further, being a person-centered (vs. expert-centered) therapist means treating our clients, whether children or adults, as experts on themselves. This is not a new concept—it is a central tenet in the work of Carl Rogers and, before that, Otto Rank. Listening to people means embracing their expertise on themselves, whether they have a chronic state of threat or not. Exercising empathy and accepting what clients have to say do not mean we must agree with everything they say; rather, we provide a safe holding space for a person on the spectrum to exist without judgment. Clients in a state of threat tend to be extremely accurate in identifying what does and does not make them feel safe.

Much like a traumatized nervous system, which overactivates the sympathetic and dorsal vagal systems, a condition like autism affects all areas of human functioning. Thus it is important as a therapist working with folks on the autism spectrum to understand how this pervasive lack of a sense of safety affects such key areas as executive function, memory recall, body awareness, and alexithymia. We will also look at ways to measure the effects of interventions that address these effects.

Executive Function

Russell Barkley is widely considered to be one of the foremost leaders in the study of EXECUTIVE FUNCTIONING (EF). Barkley and Murphy define EF as "self-regulation across time for the attainment of one's goals (self-interests), often in the context of others" (Barkley & Murphy, 2010; Barkley, 2010, 2011, 2012).

This ability is often impaired across the life course of an autistic person: an estimated 41–78% of persons on the spectrum are affected (Lynch et al., 2017). Barkley identifies five areas that comprise EF: time management, organization and problem solving, self-restraint, self-motivation, and emotional regulation.

In a meta-analysis on HRV and EF, increased sympathetic and decreased parasympathetic nervous system activity correlated with worse cognitive performance in areas primarily associated with EF (Forte et al., 2019). That is, individuals who were in threat states struggled to do things like organize, problem solve, be patient or wait their turn, control their emotions, and be mindful of time compared to those who were not.

EF was long thought to be associated solely with the prefrontal cortex. However, Barkley's model posits a multifaceted cross-temporal-lobe functionality in the neurocognitive processes involved. Barkley cites several studies to indicate that only a small sample of patients with attention-deficit/hyperactivity disorder or frontal lobe disorder score in the impaired range on EF tests, which leads one to conclude that EF is a whole-nervous-system process, not a function of a singular brain region (Barkley et al., 2011; Jonsdottir et al., 2006; Willcutt et al., 2005). Thus while the nervous system moves toward the sympathetic and dorsal vagal systems, time management, organization, self-restraint, emotional regulation, and motivation improve. As Forte et al. (2019) showed, cognitive performance in areas associated with EF goes out the window when threat levels are increased. In short, being chronically in a dorsal or sympathetic state might explain why a person with autism may have increased rates of EF dysfunction.

Discussion and recommendations. When a therapist begins work with a patient with a hyperaroused nervous system (like those on the autism spectrum), an EF assessment will show clients how their EF skills compare to others in areas like emotional regulation, and how their rating might change over time. I recommend using Barkley's DEFICITS IN EXECUTIVE FUNCTIONING SCALE, which has separate versions for children and adolescents and for adults (Barkley 2010, 2012). This resource contains both a short and a long form to rate time management, organization, self-restraint, emotional regulation, and motivation. For children this form is to be completed by parents, and the adult form is a self-report Likert scale. These scores are then compiled and compared against median scores by age and gender percentiles, akin to growth charts for EF, based

on percentile: *not clinically concerning, borderline clinically concerning, mild deficiency, moderate deficiency,* and *severe impairment.* Having a codified measurement
that is normed for age and gender allows the therapist to conceptualize for clients where their own or their children's skills are in comparison to others. It also
allows pre/post testing to measure growth over time. Barkley recommends that
growth of one standard deviation in percentiles ensures that the result is from
intervention, not just by chance. Thus it is useful if a clinician is trying to show
change over time to funders like insurance agencies. Many interventions can be
paired nicely to meet concerns in all five EF areas, time management, organization, self-restraint, emotional regulation, and motivation.

Memory Recall

In Barkley's theory the ability to retrieve information requires EF to inhibit
external stimuli that might disrupt memory recall. This evolutionary ability to
inhibit other stimuli is necessary in social domains where these tasks are done in
collaboration or even competition with others. So, for instance, when someone
is playing a trivia game and winning depends on fast recall, success will depend
on the person being happy, joyful, and flexible—that is, in a ventral vagal state.
As Forte et al. (2019) demonstrated, being in this state allows access to the EF to
inhibit external stimuli and perform better on tasks like memory recall. Thus,
in someone who mostly occupies dorsal and sympathetic states, we expect to see
challenges with memory recall, due to inhibition of nervous system processes
that enable energy to be redirected this way.

This discussion of memory recall highlights the adaptive information processing model frequently used in Francine Shapiro's (2001) EYE MOVEMENT DESEN-
SITIZATION AND REPROCESSING (EMDR), described in this chapter. The word
"trauma" occurs throughout this discussion, but for a polyvagal model of autism
this definition needs to be widened. TRAUMA in the context of this model of
practice refers not only to ADVERSE CHILDHOOD EXPERIENCES (ACEs) but also to
specific sensory experiences that are highly dysregulating to an individual's nervous system (e.g., explosions for persons with hypersensitivity to sound). Here
both types of experiences fall under the umbrella term "trauma."

ADAPTIVE INFORMATION PROCESSING THEORY suggests that the normal
processing of information by the brain is disrupted during a traumatic event,
causing the brain to lose certain information it would normally integrate into
long-term memory and thus creating a maladaptive memory (Hill, 2020).

EMDR helps reprocess and store these memories in a more organized way, thus decreasing PTSD symptoms (Shapiro, 2014). Typically we store our memories in the memory recall portion of the brain as a combination of sensory information about the universe and logical information. However, during adverse experiences, including ACEs, information is stored improperly and the logical information does not get processed, in a non-encoded way that occupies the amygdala, which leads to increased activation of the sympathetic and dorsal systems. Information that is not properly stored does not integrate into long-term memory, resulting in activation of fight/flight and freeze/collapse systems and increased somatic complaints.

When it comes to treating trauma, for instance, from an EMDR standpoint, the practitioner follows a rather lengthy protocol to determine when and how to use bilateral stimulation to reduce the emotional reactivity of the memory, thus allowing new logical information to be stored with the sensory information taken in at the time of the traumatic events unfolding. For BILATERAL STIMULATION, practitioners stimulate both the right and left hemispheres of the brain, alternately, while a memory is brought to the surface (typically a traumatic one) and reprocessed to reduce its reactivity. Bilateral stimulation can involve the practitioner using a hand moving from right to left in intervals for visual stimulation, the sound of buzzing devices in left and right ears, or the feel of tapping on left and right hands, to repeatedly activate both hemispheres of the brain. Although the details behind the effect are still under study, this process reduces activation of the memory network in the amygdala and reintroduces logical information, shifting the memory network. This process of reprogramming memories into new ones uses a process called NEUROPLASTICITY, which parallels the concept of NEURODIVERSITY. A thorough discussion of this parallel and its implications is beyond the scope of what can be covered meaningfully here, so instead I focus on developing effective therapeutic strategies informed by understandings generated from these concepts.

If we think about what happens in EMDR in polyvagal terms, we can explore what happens to EF skills during a traumatic memory, as Shields et al. (2016) and Forte et al. (2019) show in their experiments on the effects of threat states on cognitive performance. Consider a young female coming to see you to work on a memory of being beaten by her mother, which now results in her avoiding any sexual contact when she is sexually aroused by a romantic partner. An EMDR therapist will ask her to call to mind a memory of when she was beaten by her mother, evaluate the distress level of the memory at the onset of the work, and then ask her to focus on her hand moving slowly back and forth. The therapist asks her to again rate the distress level of the memory, which gradually declines. As it declines, in an unprompted way more information is recalled that was not previously available. Over sessions the missing unconscious safety information (physical contact is safe) and other logical memories that become available will gradually be reintegrated into long-term memory. Ideally, decreased distress levels and increased stress tolerance to this memory will allow her to increase her comfort with sexual contact as that logical information returns. In short, it becomes increasingly possible for this young woman to access the logical information of situations of safety and engage in meaningful romantic activity with consenting partners. The ability to access key EF skills to separate and evaluate stimuli is a cognitive task that is substantially reduced by poorly stored information.

Discussion and recommendations. Memory recall is often lumped together with EF when considering treatment approaches. Shapiro's model of adaptive information processing does not explain the role of sensory information in EMDR, but it does offer a way to think about how information received by the body is stored in both regulated and dysregulated states. Information processing requires prioritizing input from both inside the human body and the outside environment through the seven senses (the basic 5, plus interoception and proprioception). Because EMDR can be effective with a range of external stimulation, we know that visual, auditory, and tactile pathways are involved in information processing and memory formation (Shapiro, 2001). Lanius and Bergmann (2014) hypothesize that sensory awareness and stimulation undergird the adaptive information processing theory, further suggesting that an understanding of memory encoding must make room for the integration of both ordered and disordered sensory information.

The adaptive information processing model has been expanded to include how the nervous system appears to treat sensory dysregulation, that is, an event that disrupts memory storage. And while this text does not specifically endorse the use of EMDR, there is evidence to suggest that it works in treating trauma for adolescents with (and without) intellectual disabilities (e.g., an IQ of 50–85) and adults with autism (Leuning et al., 2023; Lobregt-van Buuren et al., 2019; Mevissen et al., 2020). The integration of EMDR-type protocols is beyond the scope of this book, but the research that underlies this type of intervention is central to the discussion here. The adaptive information processing model provides a helpful frame for understanding how memory can or cannot be recalled, depending on vagal state, which poorly processed sensory information disrupts. The key tenet is that *we can explain through the polyvagal model how memory recall is disrupted by traumatic events and dysregulating sensory experiences, which then results in EF deficits.* It may or may not be useful for clinicians to provide such an explanation to clients; it may help them understand how information retrieval is disrupted when one's sympathetic nervous system is frequently activated, and how this might interact with tasks like taking tests, performance on the job, or completing homework.

Body Awareness

While traditionally EMDR can be thought of as a full body therapy, the neural exercises I set forth here are more closely linked to its cousin, SENSORIMOTOR PSYCHOTHERAPY. Therapists within this tradition seek to understand pathways that clients' bodies use to organize information and organize the world, often referred to as the FIVE MICE (Ogden et al., 2006): the five senses, movement, inner sensations, cognitions, and emotions (Table 2.1). In the treatment of trauma, sensorimotor psychotherapists first prioritize treatment of bodily core organizers (the five senses, movements, and inner sensations), followed by emo-

Table 2.1: Five core organizers for body, emotion, and cognition (Ogden et al., 2006)

1. *Five-sense perception:* Sight, smell, sound, touch, and taste information (exteroceptive senses)

2. *Movement:* Gross and fine motor skills and micromovements, either consciously coordinated or unconsciously created

3. *Inner body sensations:* Physical feelings that are created from the various systems in the body and give feedback about internal states (interoceptive senses)

4. *Cognition:* Meanings made about self, others, and the world

5. *Emotion:* The more subtle aspects of human experience that shift, like positive and negative tones

tional experience, and finally cognitive information. This therapeutic approach can be thought of as prioritizing the body-based information, rather than a Cartesian approach highlighting cognition and storytelling, in order to access the body's natural ability to provide wisdom and healing.

Beliefs and cognition are an important part of this approach; Chapter 8 (Figure 8.1) highlights the work of Deb Dana (2018) on how to connect these to body awareness. This approach is also highly compatible with literature on doing cognitive behavioral therapy (e.g., Gaus, 2018). Bodily awareness among autistic individuals has long been suspected to be disordered. From a Sensorimotor Psychotherapy perceptive this refers to *inner bodily sensations*; a non-trauma therapist might think of *interoceptive and proprioceptive awareness*.

Two major studies have articulated more formal empirical evidence that autistic persons often have impaired INTEROCEPTIVE AWARENESS, the sense of what is happening within their own body, internally, via felt sensations. Fiene and Brownlow (2015) compared body awareness and thirst awareness between those diagnosed with ASD ($n = 74$; 36 males) and a control group ($n = 228$; 53 males, 1 unspecified). Both groups completed the Body Awareness Questionnaire and the Thirst Awareness Questionnaire, two common and reliable measures of interoception. Adults with ASD reported clinically significantly lower levels of body awareness and thirst awareness than their nonautistic peers, suggesting considerable difference in interoceptive awareness.

In the second study, Cabrera et al. (2017) used a much smaller sample size to explore how interoceptive experiences influence emotions in persons on the autism spectrum. They found reduced interoceptive accuracy in the ASD versus the control group. Impairment of interoceptive awareness in individuals on the spectrum is consistent with not being in a ventral vagal state. Tuning out body awareness may be a stress response.

Discussion and recommendations. In keeping with a polyvagal model of autism, a polyvagal tool to measure changes in a client's bodily awareness that is both valid and reliable will be useful to track progress in therapy. Integrated Listening Systems carries a free version of the BODY PERCEPTION QUESTIONNAIRE (BPQ), created by Stephen Porges, Jacek Kolacz, and Logan Holmes, that can be accessed by a simple Google search. The short form has a manual explaining how to measure change in bodily awareness. The BPQ has been validated and tested in multiple countries and languages, demonstrating psychometric reliability and rigor in both clinical and nonclinical settings (Cabrera et al., 2017).

The BPQ gives clinicians a clearer picture of the nervous system of someone with autism by breaking it down into body awareness and autonomic reactivity, which is further broken down into SUB- AND SUPRA-DIAPHRAGMATIC REACTIV-ITY, referring to the responses of the autonomically innervated organs above (supra-) the diaphragm and of the autonomically innervated gastrointestinal organs below (sub-) the diaphragm. While it is not as widely popularized in the field of occupational therapy as the COMPREHENSIVE ASSESSMENT OF INTERO-CEPTIVE AWARENESS, by Kelly Mahler (2016), the BPQ has been shown to be both validated and reliable, whereas the psychometric properties of the Compre-hensive Assessment have not yet been validated (as of December 2023).

Alexithymia

ALEXITHYMIA was originally defined as "(1) difficulty identifying feelings, dif-ficulty differentiating among the range of common affects, and distinguishing feelings and bodily sensations of emotional arousal, (2) difficulty finding words to describe feelings to other people, (3) constricted imaginal processes, as evi-denced by a paucity or absence of fantasy referable to drives or feelings, and (4) a thought content characterized by preoccupation with the minute details of external events" (Nemiah et al., 1976). Alexithymia is thought to affect nearly half of autistic adults (Kinnaird et al., 2019), so it is a common topic in research on the autistic experience with emotions. However, it is unclear from this research whether it is a static or modifiable condition.

Studies have provided mixed answers to this question. Some (e.g., de Groot et al., 1995; Grabe et al., 2008) argue that alexithymia is a state-dependent condi-tion, but their results largely rely on underlying trauma or illness, usually mea-sured by changes in scores on anxiety and depression. Others (e.g., Tolmunen et al., 2011) that used large-scale longitudinal studies found relatively few changes in the general population, which remained largely alexithymic over a period of 11 years. A particularly relevant study (Panayiotou et al., 2015) involved a seven-week trial of daily cognitive behavioral therapy in 163 individuals with obsessive-compulsive disorders. Depression scores improved, and alexithymia levels decreased per TAS-20 scores (see below), which was mediated by decreased lev-els of avoidance. Thus, although how much alexithymia can be modified is not yet understood, there is hope for increased levels of emotional regulation among individuals with autism if the emotional coding process can be improved.

Another complexity to measuring changes in alexithymia in autistic adults is that the most widely researched tool is not necessarily a valid scientific instrument. The TORONTO ALEXITHYMIA SCALE-20 (TAS-20) is copyrighted and cannot be distributed here because of intellectual property rights; however, it can be purchased from its creator, Dr. Graeme Taylor. Answers from the TAS-20 can also be entered into the 8-item General Alexithymia Factor Score Calculator (see Williams, 2021) created by Zack Williams of Vanderbilt University (Williams & Gotham, 2021). This tool accounts for the psychometric difficulties of using of the TAS-20 to measure alexithymia levels in autistic adults, giving more reliable results by winnowing down the twenty questions to the eight considered psychometrically valid in the ASD population.

Discussion and recommendations. While alexithymia is a classic psychodynamic concept that is gaining in validity, clinicians must choose whether and how they wish to measure it. Alexithymia is a useful concept, and a number of measures examine it, but current research has validated only the TAS-20 for translation to the General Alexithymia Factor 8 Calculator, suggesting other measures of alexithymia, while valid for most populations, are not necessarily valid for ASD. Present research is highly inconclusive about the effectiveness of interventions, so whether to introduce this concept to those on the autism spectrum is a difficult decision. We do not know whether a person on the spectrum with alexithymia will ever change, and expectations must be set accordingly. It would be wonderful to be able to promise clients that they can fully access the energetic experience of emotional life, but there is no guarantee that this is in fact an achievable goal. However, if this is understood by clients on the front end, and the measurement of alexithymia is integrated as a tertiary measure of change in emotional awareness, it can be a useful tool.

AWARENESS AND MOVEMENT FORWARD

It is often said that individuals in Silicon Valley are more likely to be on the autism spectrum—that tech geeks, with their social awkwardness, focused interests in technology, and poor communication skills, have raised the ASD level of the local population. While that may or may not be true, it calls to mind the wisdom of Janina Fisher, another pioneer in the field of Sensorimotor Psychotherapy, in her talk at the Minnesota Clinical Hypnosis Society: "We cannot accept ourselves because we are locked in an internal struggle between yearning for acceptance and self-rejection" (Fisher, 2022). Inability to accept the self often reflects a logical part trying to ensure an autistic person's survival, by rationalizing the pain they experience rather than feeling it in a more energetic and body-based way. To understand this next part we need to conceptualize the human consciousness through a more disjointed lens, in internal family systems therapy they refer to these as parts. Manager parts, that keep things going to avoid

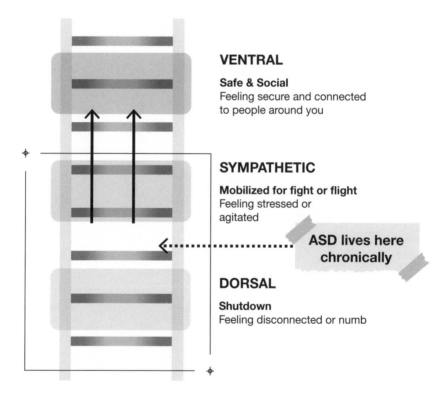

Figure 2.1: Autistic nervous systems alternate between fight/flight and freeze/ collapse (boxed area). The goal of therapy is to help the nervous system experience safety (arrows), so clients can learn to flip the vagal switch on their own.
Source: Adapted from POLYVAGAL FLIP CHART: UNDERSTANDING THE SCIENCE OF SAFETY by Deb Dana. Copyright © by Deborah A. Dana. Used by permission of W. W. Norton & Company, Inc.

the pain, protector parts, which protect exile or child parts from the pain, and exiles, which are the parts of us that carry our most painful memories.

In parts language, we might consider this a conflict between two protectors— parts of the self that ensure our survival by shielding younger parts from the pain we experience. Being in the sympathetic and dorsal levels of the ladder makes it difficult to experience feelings with any level of clarity. Reliance on logic that in turn is not that logical at all—it is not grounded in a ventral state of being—and an unfelt sense of safety may be why clients with ASD find it difficult to identify feelings and describe their internal experience to others.

CHAPTER 3

The Sympathetic Nervous System, Dorsal Vagal System, and Autism

··

At times it will be necessary to have the courage to tell of very intimate experiences.

VIKTOR FRANKL

THE FIGHT, THE FLIGHT, AND THE COLLAPSE

Animals in the mammalian kingdom have a number of responses that help them survive. Consider relationships between predator and prey. The lion in the African savannah is expected to stalk her prey. And the antelope is expected to use its two most basic survival strategies to avoid death: first flight, trying to outrun the lion, and then fight, trying to use its horns to impale the lion. Both of these strategies are evolutionary adaptations that antelope for millennia have used to survive.

When these strategies of fight and flight fail, the lion has captured her next meal. The antelope has tried with all its might to fight off and escape its predator, but in the end it collapses. We humans do the same when our first lines of defense—flight and fight—have failed: we shut down.

We most often think about these animal responses in terms of survival; we tend to think of human beings in terms of trauma. In some traumatic situations, unlike the antelope shutting down, in humans the collapse response actually enables survival. For instance, when a person is being raped, their ability to dissociate or collapse might actually help keep them alive and survive the horrific experience. Rape involves a person forcing someone to meet that person's bestial desires, usually under threat of violence, even threat of death, to the victim or their loved ones. In such a scenario, zoning out can be an effective coping strategy, but not in the context of a chronic sense of threat.

AUTISM AND THREAT RESPONSE

During a state of fight, flight, or collapse, it is exceptionally common to experience stubbornness or cognitive inflexibility, difficulty reading and regulating feelings, difficulty making eye contact, and difficulty with reciprocal communication. In autism, as in its fellow mental health diagnosis posttraumatic stress disorder (PTSD), the nervous system is in a chronic threat state. And persons with autism who have experienced no trauma activate these same threat pathways—perhaps due to issues with sensory integration or stress, or some other, unknown cause. We do know that anyone who is feeling threatened behaves much like a person who struggles with eye contact.

If a child has difficulty making eye contact and reading social cues, your first thought might be autism. But as we have begun to explore, a child like this, from a polyvagal perspective, is continually experiencing fight/flight or collapse responses.

POLYVAGAL THEORY–INFORMED MODEL OF AUTISM SPECTRUM DISORDER

Hearts of those who are on the spectrum beat faster than do hearts of those who are not. We also see challenges with social interactions, restrictive and repetitive patterns of interest or behavior, and difficulties with social nuances of communication. And when we look at those without autism who are in a threatening situation, we see challenges very similar to those faced by folks on the spectrum. For instance, Lischke et al. (2018) found that people with ASD showed increased sympathetic activity compared to those without, and struggled with empathy.

It is often brought up in criminal trials of autistic individuals how they lack empathy. This same trait is often seen with severe addictions, and those with extreme trauma in their past. The evidence suggests these may all reflect a body constantly on high alert, unable to take in emotional information that might tell the nervous system to stop.

Alexithymia is often linked with lack of empathy. Kinnaird et al. (2019) posit that autistic adults have a prevalence rate of 1 in 2, which would explain why so many folks with autism struggle socially. In three studies involving people with lower ventral vagal regulation, as indexed by HRV, they struggled with facial expression control (Porges, 2005; Porges et al., 2013, 2014). In simple terms, the vagus nerve connects our heart to our socially responsive muscles (eyes, mouth, ears, etc.). If the vagus nerve is shut down, we might expect our social response systems to shut down too.

While it may be considered normative or privileged to presume eye contact reflects neurotypical behaviors, science demands that we have norms against which to measure things. For the purposes of this book, eye contact is considered normative, but this is likely very contextually situated. In an experiment comparing those with and without PTSD, Steuwe et al. (2014) measured gaze aversion using functional MRI in 32 participants (16 healthy, and 16 with a diagnosis of PTSD). Those with PTSD were far more likely to avert gaze to images regardless of emotional presentation. When you consider that those with PTSD have lower HRV during episodes of trauma flashbacks (Porges, S. & S. W., 2023; Dana, 2018; Hughes, 2012; Siegel, 1999, 2023), such struggles with eye contact in those with low HRV (e.g., those with poor vagal efficiency) may be a threat response.

Some may consider direct gaze painful or socially unacceptable; others may consider it ableist to assume that direct gaze should be considered the norm. ABLEIST refers to viewing the world through the lens of people who are fully capable of doing most if not all functions of the human body, and building the world around that. However, the science of interpersonal neurobiology provides support for this view. Across three studies, individuals with autism with low HRV (or poor vagal efficiency) also struggled with eye contact (Porges et al., 2005, 2013, 2014). Another study (Patriquin et al., 2019), led by the director of research at Menninger Clinic, found in children without ASD that those with higher HRV possessed better social skills, joint attention skills, and language abilities. In keeping with adaptive information processing theory and Barkley's theories of executive function

(EF) skills, those with higher levels of HRV might demonstrate improved memory recall, gaze-holding, and joint attention skills. Succinctly put, if we start with the body and follow its natural functions, it should come as no surprise that those with autism consistently demonstrate EF deficits.

Thus, it comes as no surprise that EMDR, a manualized form of ADAPTIVE INFORMATION PROCESSING THEORY, might be used to treat PTSD, given the diagnostic overlap of restrictive, repetitive behaviors. From an assessment perspective, one of the most difficult areas to differentiate (covered in more depth in later chapters) is the overlap of PTSD and ASD, in part because restrictive, repetitive patterns of interest and behavior can be used as coping mechanisms in both cases. With respect to diagnosis of autism, Vasile et al. (2022) looked at 214 autism diagnoses of 5- to 16-year-olds using the ADOS-2 (the gold standard of autism measurement) and found a rate of 34% false positives and 1% false negatives, primarily because of the presence of trauma. Maddox et al. (2017), in a similar study of 75 ASD assessments of adults with psychosis, found a false-positive rate of 30% with the ADOS-2. Additionally, Mazefsky and Oswald (2006) explored validity of ADOS-2 and ADI-R and found a rate of 30% false diagnosis for ASD.

As described in preceding chapters, this murky issue of diagnosis reflects how some coping patterns might also be stimming-type behaviors or, as the ADOS-2 terms it, restrictive, repetitive patterns of interest and behaviors. These ways that patients organize their experience might be highly disruptive to others, for example, a fascination with pinball that makes one mute, as The Who describe in their 1969 rock opera *Tommy*. And even while there are questions as to why, Alba et al. (2019) found in adults with higher levels of HRV activity that HRV significantly correlated with the ability to remain cognitively flexible. In short, beats per minute correlate with how flexible and open to change a person can remain: low beats per minute would be able to remain more flexible than someone with higher beats per minute (e.g., a person with ASD or PTSD).

In the Polyvagal Theory–informed model of autism, mechanisms that have long been understood as disorders of neurodevelopment can instead be thought of as DURABLE: a person on the spectrum cannot leave the chronic state of sympathetic and dorsal vagal system activation without some level of work, and even with work can remain unchanging at points in development. Decreased HRV leads to autonomic states like fight/flight or collapse, rooted in the sympathetic and dorsal vagal systems, being durably, chronically active.

When we think about bodily responses of the autonomic nervous system, we see very little difference between PTSD, obsessive-compulsive disorder (OCD), and autism. All are expressions of a dampened social engagement system and an increasingly activated state of threat detection. However, there are some significant differences, as discussed in Chapter 5.

RESTRICTIVE AND REPETITIVE PATTERNS OF THOUGHT AND BEHAVIOR

A key characteristic of the *DSM-5-TR* definition of autism is "restrictive and repetitive patterns of thoughts and behaviors." This is distinctly different from the symptoms of OCD. According to the International Obsessive Compulsive Disorder Foundation (n.d.), obsessions are "thoughts, images or impulses that occur over and over again and feel outside of the person's control. Individuals with OCD do not want to have these thoughts and find them disturbing." Similar to the case in autism, these thought patterns and behaviors restrict individuals from paying attention to competing interests. However, there is a key distinction between these two conditions: OCD is characterized by intrusive thoughts or unwanted thoughts or impulses, unlike in autism, where the patterns of thought and behavior actually are desired, often are considered a special interest. And in many cases these repetitive thoughts and behaviors can actually become beautiful and wonderful adaptations. Take Fender, a seven-year-old client with autism who was obsessed with cars. Unlike most seven-year-olds, Fender was highly aggressive toward others, to the point where he got kicked out of a day treatment program. Also unlike other seven-year-olds, Fender is able to build a car engine.

Fender demonstrates how a restrictive, repetitive pattern of behaviors can manifest as a beautiful adaptation despite the presence of other, maladaptive behaviors. Fender's love of car engines is not intrusive; rather, it is born of love and desire, distinctly different than a compulsion, which has an intrusive component. Thus, some in diagnostic work consider these conditions to be distinctly different (Santore et al., 2020) and unlikely to co-occur. In contrast, if we think about restrictive and repetitive interests and behaviors as expressions of frequent activation of the sympathetic or the dorsal vagus system, this suggests that clients with autism might be able to modulate their cognitive flexibility. Lower levels of HRV, as is often witnessed in autistic persons, might be correlated with this maladaptive form of repetitive interest, but cognitive flexibility might increase along with higher levels of HRV. Williams et al. (2017) found exactly this: employees with lower HRV were more likely to have maladaptive ruminations, while those with higher HRV had more cognitive flexibility.

It would seem from this research that a person's restrictive and repetitive patterns of thought and behavior are modulated by their CARDIO-INHIBITORY PATHWAYS, whether they are diagnosed with autism or OCD. While this is still the subject of further research, it represents a theoretically interesting and clinically straightforward way to help our autistic patients become less functionally inhibited by maladaptive ruminations.

Discussion and recommendations. OCD and ASD tend to be markedly similar in their bodily expression. While these two disorders are not mutually exclusive, they represent two different types of restrictive and repetitive patterns of behavior: in OCD these are more intrusive and unwanted, whereas in ASD they are often wanted and desirable even if maladaptive.

With respect to assessment, it may be tempting to launch into an either/or analysis with a client regarding ASD and OCD symptoms. However, exploring what clients with autism experience, in an open and curious way, acknowledges that they are the expert on themselves. Thus, begin with open-ended questions, for example,

A. Can you tell me about these restrictive or repetitive patterns of behaviors?
B. How long have you noticed they are present?
C. Do these patterns cause you some kind of distress?

As therapist our role is to provide nonjudgmental space for inquiry and openness. Questions such as "Are these patterns causing you some kind of distress?" usually elicit a more thoughtful response on the part of the listener.

DEFICITS IN SOCIAL COMMUNICATION

People with autism demonstrate difficulties with social interaction, such as those depicted in the movies *Rain Man* and *Good Will Hunting* and television shows like *Atypical*. My life as a teenager with autism was similar in some ways to these popular depictions. I struggled in high school with dating and with the social cues involved in reading whether or not someone was attracted to me. One might say that I was chronically in fight/flight (sympathetic nervous system activation) and collapse (dorsal vagal system activation). Intimidated by the opposite sex, I rarely risked interaction—I dated one girl, I think for a period of three months. Taking a risk is a choice made from a sense of safety, something I never had the chance to develop and that I continue to struggle with to this day.

As a teen, my body could not achieve a safe state. As an adult living on my own, however, having relationships and experiences away from the unsafe-feeling environment of my geographic home created enough momentary experiences to allow me to temporarily shift into safe states. I've been able to enjoy SAFETY for brief periods of my life while with partners like Jess and Stella. When people on the spectrum are in a frequent state of threat, it is much more difficult for them to receive safety cues involved in romance, such as prolonged gaze, changes in vocal tones, and light touch. Thus, the work of a therapist treating an autistic client involves helping that client slow down disorganized, adaptive strategies and find moments and experiences of safety. We must recognize these less-than-conscious processes that may have been useful on the African savannah but are less so in our industrialized world. It becomes the work of therapy to begin to call forth and create moments of safety in the therapeutic space, so that clients can safely experiment with how this experience feels and how to carry it forward into daily life.

A key distinction that we as clinicians must make with and for our autistic clients is that autism is not necessarily the result of childhood trauma. Genetics, deficits in sensory integration, and complications during birth could also be precipitating factors leading to the chronic state of threat activation by the autonomic nervous system.

Discussion and recommendations. While the bodily experience of the autonomic nervous system is similar for autism, OCD, and PTSD, these three diagnoses are distinctly different regarding assessment and treatment. Clinicians who specialize in treating autism are often asked, "Do I or don't I have autism?" It's a difficult question to answer because of the many common symptoms between ASD and OCD, such as shifts in mood, sensory sensitivity, disruptions in EF skills, and self-harm. However, the implications are far more severe for an autism diagnosis than for an OCD or PTSD diagnosis. Both PTSD and OCD have a variety of treatments and potential cures; ASD, in contrast, is the opposite, according to modern medical science and insurers. In the view of Medicaid, for instance, autism is a lifelong and enduring diagnosis, for which often applied behavioral analysis (ABA) treatments are reimbursed.

A study by the prestigious A. J. Drexel Autism Institute reported that from 2005 to 2015 there was a 327% jump in disability determinations granted to children with ASD (Anderson et al., 2020). Anderson's team, too, encountered difficulties in teasing out differential diagnoses, and since clinicians will likely encounter the same rise in requests for assessment, it may be worthwhile to be trained in a validated psychometric tool like the Autism Diagnostic Observation Scale-2 (ADOS-2), the Autism Mental Status Exam, or the Social Responsiveness Scale. Accurate distinctions still must be made within the context of existing stereotypes about autism, for example, that it is a lifelong and enduring condition. And although from a polyvagal lens this may not be the case, which affects how we treat and work with clients with ASD, this view still pervades systems like education, social security, and Medicaid-based state programs. This puts therapists in a precarious position of needing to prepare clients for the potentially lifelong discrimination they may face with their diagnosis while simultaneously increasing their hope for new and enduring outcomes.

ASSESSMENT AND MOVING FORWARD

When we consider ASD from a polyvagal perspective, the tone of the assistance we provide changes, from trying to locate, or become, an expert on autism to finding a way to engage the very nervous system in front of us in a way that can bring relief. In my clinical practice it really is this simple: goals are set by individuals, not by diagnoses, which can inform treatment but should not define one's identity. If we think about people with autism as humans with a nervous system in a state of threat, their overarching need becomes much simpler: an enduring feeling of safety.

They need us to be kind.

CHAPTER 4

Engaging the Autistic Nervous System

··

You only need to breathe mindfully and smile to your habit energy: "Oh, I got pulled away by that again." When you can recognize habit energies this way, they lose their hold on you, and you're free once again to live peacefully and happily in the present.

THICH NHAT HANH

Autism is characterized largely in two ways: restrictive and repetitive interests, and difficulties with the social aspects of communications. As the first three chapters have described, the activation of threat states is a natural, unconscious physical and emotional response by the body to perceived threat. And while the autistic body may be under no physical threat, there is a felt sense of threat: the whole world is a threat. So, as a person on the spectrum, as a therapist, as a parent or educator of a person on the spectrum, what can you do to support yourself or someone on the spectrum?

The answer is kindness. This may seem simplistic at first glance, but there are a number of research-based ways to evince kindness. If we assume that autism is a chronic state of threat, and that those with chronic states of threat demonstrate lower heart rate variability (HRV), or more resting heart beats per minute, these are the same thing taken with different instruments and in different conditions. HRV is taken under lab conditions with an instrument like the *beat pack*, and pulse is taken in clinical settings, usually with an oximeter, and they tend to be calculated in the span of a minute. Patients with lower HRV exhibit the quintessential symptoms of autism: mental inflexibility and difficulties with nonverbal and verbal social communication.

The chapters in Parts 2 and 3 of this book explore interventions designed from a polyvagal perspective to reduce cognitive inflexibility and deficits in social communication. These simple interventions need to be applied with an "autism-friendly" set of values that provide a framework within which to treat clients with autism. These values are derived from both actual autistic patient experience and such established clinical practices as Sensorimotor Psychotherapy, mindfulness, motivational interviewing, and social work pedagogy. The strategies I outline in this book are informed by similar values.

THE VALUES UNDERLYING NEURAL EXERCISES

While technique is undeniably important, it is the spirit of the practice that is perhaps the most impactful—not just the skills employed to forming relationships with autistic clients and their autonomic nervous system but also the felt space of relational alchemy between the autistic person and therapist, caregiver, or educator. This spirit, embodied in the values described here, is at the heart of this practice.

Like other approaches before it, neural exercises are indebted to therapies of yesteryear, building on traditions of mindfulness, Sensorimotor Psychotherapy, Polyvagal Theory, social work pedagogy, and motivational interviewing. The values underlying these psychotherapy traditions represent a distinct departure from systems of conditional regard used in such approaches as applied behavioral analysis (ABA) and early forms of cognitive behavior therapy; later forms of cognitive behavioral therapy, like Linehan's dialectical behavioral therapy and Hayes's acceptance and commitment therapy, have moved away from the stimulus-response relationship. But neural exercises, like their predecessors, are distinguished by their more mindful and holistic approach to the autistic person as experiencing a set of core symptoms caused by a dysregulated ventral vagal system, with a frequent and almost uncontrollable threat state activation.

As noted in the Introduction, psychotherapeutic traditions rely on the alliance between therapist and client, which can be challenging with clients who struggle to relate to others. The strategies offered here, which can help form strong relationships with such clients, are founded on these seven values:

1. Kindness
2. Quality
3. Openness
4. Generosity
5. Respect
6. Organicity
7. Mindfulness

This chapter begins to unpack these values in the context of treatment for autistic clients to help them work with their core symptoms.

♡ Kindness

KINDNESS, here, refers to responding gently to our clients and facilitating a spirit of ease; this is achieved by remaining attuned to our own autonomic nervous system as well as to that of our client. Perhaps what separates neural exercises from its predecessors is this spirit of kindness. It is not merely enough to approach attunement with a spirit of agreement; rather, we need a spirit of gentle ease. When asked to comment on how she encourages clinicians to engage in gentleness, Pat Ogden told me, "It's about embodying non-violence and organicity" (personal communication, May, 23, 2023). Although there may be some instances when being blunter may help convey a message, even this must be done in a way that the therapeutic alliance can support and the message can be received. While it is impossible to *completely* attune to our autistic clients, with simplicity and calmness we may be able to evoke the hope in our patients that they need to achieve what they so fundamentally seek.

Clients with ASD typically seek to address a functional impairment likely linked to core symptoms of autism: cognitive inflexibility or social communication deficits. Our approach to changing this self-perceived deficit must be handled with care and ease. In my own clinical experience, patients with autism often have a long history of self second-guessing, and self-esteem tends to be a challenge. Therefore, it is with the lightest touch that we must approach autistic clients who bring themselves to us. The abiding goal for the therapist is to cultivate a safe space—whether through a closed-ended question using a menu of options or with a reflective statement—necessary to support the already activated autonomic nervous system.

The use of kindness allows a different social environment to form, one the autistic self may not be accustomed to. The therapist creates a social tapestry that *invites* rather than demands—often a new way of existence for a chronically activated autonomic nervous system. This environment invites the ventral vagal system to open and the deep animal defenses of rigidity and inflexibility to lessen, in direct contrast to what this autonomic nervous system is accustomed to: negative judgment for an intense, direct communication style that is often lacking in nuance. When we meet their explicit communication style with ease and gentleness, we reduce that inner dialogue of judgment for the self's perceived social deficits. We can invite the autonomic nervous system to yield its relational defensive system so that the autistic individual can become curious, rather than judgmental, about their social experience and repetitive interests.

★ Quality

In the context of treatment, QUALITY refers to "excellence, reliability, ethics, integrity, professionalism, responsiveness to emerging evidence" (Sensorimotor Psychotherapy Institute, 2022). This modality is evidence based. To comprehend results, we rely on evidence of the psychological change our clients wish to see. Using evidence-based tools to measure integration of new knowledge is central to modulating the core symptoms of autism.

There is much talk of evidence-based practices, especially regarding reimbursement. A polyvagal view of the neurobiological origins of autism is relatively new to science. Although much evidence exists to support this approach (as we witness in Chapters 2 and 3), many states at the time of this writing do not reimburse for therapy services for autism outside of ABA. As the science of the polyvagal explanation of autism becomes better known, ideally reimbursement practices will change.

Openness

OPENNESS refers to the ability to shift from existing perspectives to new, under-explored ways of thinking (Sensorimotor Psychotherapy Institute, 2022). It stands in direct contrast to one of the core symptoms of autism: cognitive inflexibility. For any therapist working with an autistic person, it is critical to demonstrate willingness to change and to not take oneself too seriously, thus allowing the client to adopt a similar posture. The ego of the therapist cannot depend on the opinion of the autistic person; chances are that people with autism will be critical of a therapist's ability a substantial number of times. In the eyes of my own autistic clients, failing is a regular occurrence, and having communication about these failures is a key element of therapy.

It is not the client's responsibility to shape the therapist's concept of self, or to make the other person in this helping relationship feel good about themselves. Therapeutic use of self-disclosure is a valuable tool, but not for the purpose of meeting the therapist's own social needs. Therefore, openness here is about sharing stories not for the self-esteem of the therapist but, rather, to invite inquiry and critical thinking. In short, we can invite criticism and curiosity about our own clinical practice; clients with autism will surely tell us what they think went well and what didn't.

While writing this book I had the distinct pleasure of interviewing Barry Prizant, PhD, author of *Uniquely Human* and codeveloper of the SCERTS® (Social Communication, Emotional Regulation, and Transactional Support) model. In this interview we discussed this idea of meeting clients where they are in terms of development. I asked Barry,

> You are further along the arc of your career than I am, and one of the things I see you do really well is not alienate groups of people. How do you do that when you speak to both doctors and parents?

He replied,

> Respectful language is super important. I'm really careful in choosing the language I use to ensure that both parents and professionals are listening and emotionally open to what I am sharing. For instance, when I discuss

aggression, I define it very narrowly. I define it as harmful behavior directed toward another with the intention of harming another. Not all difficult or disruptive behavior resulting in harm to another is aggressive, but may reflect biological behavioral states. We don't want to be blaming a person for being extremely dysregulated. (B. Prizant, personal communication, June 5, 2023)

The careful use of language Barry describes is one of the pathways through which to embody openness, especially in terms of access to knowledge regardless of educational level. It's important to recognize the distinction between clients' intentions and their actions, which often reflect behavioral states. As therapists we must attend to and be open to our own developmental journey so that we may be open to the states and needs of our clients.

➤ Generosity

GENEROSITY can be understood as a stance that embodies "non-possessiveness, sharing, acknowledgment, collaboration, cooperation," and "giving more than you receive" (MINT, n.d.). Consider the experience of Bill Miller, creator of motivational interviewing, whom I also had the joy of interviewing for this book. Academically, Bill was trained in the world of behavior therapy and behaviorism at the University of Oregon and also in a client-centered approach to therapeutic relationships. During his third predoctoral year he was struggling to teach ABA procedures to parents seeking help with their children's behavior problems. A key experience for Bill was observing Gerald Patterson work with a family at the Oregon Research Institute. "Yes, Jerry was using the ABA methods that he wrote about," Bill said, "but he was also doing a lot more. He was a warm, engaged, funny, collaborative, compassionate human being. 'Oh *that's* how you do it!' I thought. I began practicing behavior therapy in a client-centered way, and it started working." Bill's own research soon showed that therapeutic skills like accurate empathy (a form of empathy that reflects the intended meaning of a statement) make a large difference in behavior therapy outcomes.

Behaviorism and motivational interviewing are not like apples and oranges, but more like apples and caramel. They complement each other. We can offer information or advice, but it's up to the person whether to take it in. To let go of trying to control others is to relinquish a power that we never had in the first place. (W. R. Miller, personal communication, May 22, 2023)

This relinquishment of power is probably the easiest way to understand the aspect of shared decision making that embodies the value of generosity. In other modalities like ABA or general education, the teacher or parent is perceived as the source of EXPERTISE and the giver of advice. In the tradition of motivational interviewing, however, decision making is shared. People with autism are seen as experts on their own lives. If we lean into Bill's wisdom we will notice that behaviorism and neural exercises can coexist, one with the other, without one replacing the other. In the approach shared in this book, the therapist offers expertise in strategies for modulating autism's core symptoms—whether taken from mindfulness, motivational interviewing, aerobic exercise, Sensorimotor Psychotherapy, Polyvagal Theory, or social work pedagogy. The client, in turn, offers expertise in what they are seeking from treatment and how they want to receive it.

The therapist, while not an expert on the autistic person's life, is responsible for providing the scaffolding and collaborative context for social growth and cognitive flexibility to develop. You may recall the epigraph from Ron Kurtz (2009; as cited in Ogden, 2021) that began Chapter 2: "We are not healers. We are the context in which healing is inspired." It is the job of the helper to provide the autistic person a context within which to blossom both socially and cognitively.

Human services professionals trained in motivational interviewing are instructed to ask for permission prior to giving information and to not argue but, rather, dance with discord. For those unfamiliar with motivational interviewing, "dance with discord" refers to how discomfort is evoked when we begin to argue with others rather than let them advocate for their own reasons for change. In the same spirit of generosity, when practicing the neural exercises in this book, we give more than we take, practice humility, and seek collaboration for goal reaching while providing the scaffolding necessary for cognitive and social development.

⟩ Respect

RESPECT refers to the intentional promotion and acceptance of individual and professional diversity of experience and thought (Sensorimotor Psychotherapy Institute, 2022). The word "intentional" is important to this definition because it refers to how we need to integrate (take in information about and reflect back with some level of accuracy) the aspects of the human being before us. In the case of Mich and Mel, described below, this looks like the direct integration of things Mel shares with Mich. Other examples include valuing the person's experience within their difference in ethnicity, race, sexual orientation, gender identity, religious orientation, sensory experience of the world, and so on.

Like motivational interviewing, respect is intended to acknowledge the expertise of a wider audience on their diverse experiences. As I was writing this book at the Autism Society of Greater Wisconsin conference in 2023, I attended a talk by Island of Brilliance, a group that employs mentors to help clients with autism learn skills through creativity. Mich, one of the mentors and a grad student at the University of Wisconsin, Milwaukee, talked with me about how he embodies this autistic expertise in his work. I asked him what people with autism expertise look like in the context of his mentorship. He responded, "When I meet with students I try to focus in with them on what is important to them."

> Take my 14-year-old client [Mel]. He loved everything sports, the Brewers, the Bucks, the Packers. That was easy, he just wanted to connect over his interest in sports. . . . However, there are others like this student and his father and brother who came in. . . . He didn't trust me right away, and it took about three days for us to connect. When he started he would just sit with his dad and not really be close to me. However, after we started connecting over *Mario Party* and *Super Smash Brothers*, we really connected. I would be like, "I like Mewtwo. Who do you like?" he would reply, "I like Kirby." And gradually it became about Kirby and creating things like GIFs, posters, and illustrations about Kirby. We focused in on the thing he was interested in, which made him feel safe. (M. Dillon, personal communication, May 1, 2023)

And what I found so profound about Mich's words on respect is how inherently human they were: focus on what people are involved in and interested in—so simple and yet so profound in this field in which we as therapists are constantly searching for the next best intervention or the literature on expert models. What if we just relied on autistic wisdom just like we might with any other client?

🌳 Organicity

ORGANICITY refers to the "internal wisdom of all living systems. Thus, the therapist does not 'heal' the client; rather the healing and power and intelligence is within and each person has their own unique, mysterious, and emergent growth path" (Sensorimotor Psychotherapy Institute, 2022). Originally born from the work of Pat Ogden—and the Sensorimotor Psychotherapy Institute, "organicity" speaks to the inherent wisdom of the person. The goal for therapeutic change is not necessarily a cure for autism but, rather, a modulation of ASD's core symptoms so that the client is less distressed. In a talk she gave reflecting on organicity, Ogden quoted Herman Hesse's *Steppenwolf*:

> I can give you nothing that has not already its origins within yourself. I can throw open no picture gallery but your own. I can help make your own world visible—that is all.

She went on to say the poem "epitomizes organicity to me. . . . It recognizes the inherent health of the individual. . . . We don't see the client in terms of disease but doing the best that they can" (P. Ogden, personal communication, May 23, 2023).

I had the distinct pleasure of interviewing Sensorimotor Psychotherapy's creator for this book and asked Pat to comment on what organicity means in the context of those with developmental delays. Her answer, "Advice doesn't fit organicity. It is the wisdom of the clients that guides them to their next evolution." Then I asked, "So how do you guide parents who abuse their children?" She replied, "The art of therapy is you set up experiments in which children and parents co-create meaning" (P. Ogden, personal communication, May 23, 2023).

Organicity is a movement toward understanding individuals on the spectrum as doing their best to be flexible in the ways they know how and engaging in their social world as they see fit. It means seeing clients as a reflection of all the things that have helped shape who they are up to this point. As Ogden went on to say, "It's all about helping clients take their next step" (personal communication, May, 23, 2023). And in the context of living on the spectrum, we must ask this question, *What is the next step?*, often, and in the context of increased flexibility and increased social connectedness.

♟ Mindfulness

MINDFULNESS in this book refers both to a value and to a practice. As a value it involves encouraging present-moment awareness in both the client's and the therapist's experiences and calling attention to this present-moment awareness for the client. This principle is useful only to the extent that it is as self-directed and concerned with transference as it is other directed. Mindfulness can be thought of as a bidirectional concept to be applied in the therapeutic space. As with most therapies, what we bring into the room is just as important as what our clients bring to the therapy space. Hence, an awareness that begins in the therapist's, teacher's, or parent's own body, emotional experience, and cognitions is important to bringing present attention to someone who is in an elevated state of threat.

Mindfulness, then, becomes more than a therapeutic process. Mindfulness is an invitation for the therapist and client to be present within the moment and not to ruminate about what will be. It is an invitation to be open and safe in the room. To change maladaptive patterns, we as therapists must be completely present, despite the mind's tendency to go elsewhere. It is the challenge of bringing one's attention back to the present moment and recognizing when one's attention has been pulled away. It is both this simple and this hard.

IMPLICATIONS

The traditions that have shaped this approach to affect the visceral system stem from work that is shown to be clinically effective, and respectful of human dignity and worth. The shaping of behavior and cognitive patterns is secondary to doing it in a way that respects the autonomy of the human spirit. It is in this spirit of its predecessors, such as motivational interviewing and Sensorimotor Psychotherapy, that this work of neural exercises continues.

It would not be in keeping with this value system to say one "outgrows" autism, and it would not be kind or open-minded to do so. In keeping with the values discussed in this chapter, autism can be viewed as a modifiable set of traits that ranges in severity and presentation. Terms like "low" and "high" functioning are also not helpful or respectful. A generous view then might be to extend the idea that there are more optimal and less optimal ways to function within one's specific constellation of capabilities we now call "autism spectrum disorder."

From a polyvagal perspective, the symptoms of ASD, especially those involving struggles with cognitive flexibility and decreased social communication, must be seen as transient or changeable, and it is the task of therapy to work alongside clients with autism on their own goals in relation to reducing cognitive inflexibility and improving interpersonal social communication skills.

As both a clinician and a researcher, I share the neural exercises in this book with the hope that they will bring change for yourself and for your loved ones or students with ASD. I understand that some may be offended by the term "disorder," but it captures the experience of those who arrive at therapy—people come to therapy when life has become unmanageable, not when it is going well. I've written this book to give you a set of tools based on evidence and on clinical expertise from a polyvagal perspective, to help expand how you think about and serve people with autism spectrum disorder (Colzato et al., 2018).

PART 2

Polyvagal Theory–Informed Interventions for Cognitive Inflexibility

CHAPTER 5

Addressing Cognitive Inflexibility

Above all, when we are dealing with [trauma] we must be gentle.

PIERRE JANET, *PSYCHOLOGICAL HEALING: A HISTORICAL AND CLINICAL STUDY* (1925)

"Cognitive inflexibility" is a phrase commonly used to describe individuals on the autism spectrum. As in the example of Fender from Chapter 3, the violent seven-year-old who got kicked out of day treatment, a focus on restrictive and repetitive interests characteristic of autism has a habit of getting in the way of daily functioning. Theorists have long speculated that this rumination is somehow self-stimulatory or enjoyable to the individual with ASD. However, from a polyvagal perspective, is it also an expression of a dampened social engagement system that makes it more difficult to be flexible and creative.

Highly profitable companies in the United States like Hershey's, Coca-Cola, and Apple often employ organizational psychologists to help their workers achieve greater productivity, using strategies from positive psychology. FLOW, as defined by originator Mihály Csíkszentmihályi (n.d.), is "a state of deep, effortless involvement." Strategies like flow, or letting workers get lost in their work, are widely employed in many ways (Weintraub et al., 2021). However, seen through the neural exercises proposed in this book, these strategies ultimately do very little to draw out the most creative aspects of a person, by not leaning into safety instead of threat. Creativity requires a FELT SENSE OF SAFETY, which is impossible in a workplace environment driven by productivity and generation of profits—in an environment full of threat, individuals struggle to come up with new solutions. Similarly, a ruminating child will struggle to come up with answers or creative solutions at school under the pressure of threat of failure.

RUMINATION, as used throughout this book, refers to restrictive, repetitive patterns of thought or behavior, but more specifically thoughts. These patterns of thought, however beautiful and intensely satisfying to the person with autism, can become unmanageable and cause a fair amount of discomfort for those around them. At this point these intense interests might be considered maladaptive expressions of a dampened ventral vagal circuit. What can we do to help folks with autism reduce these maladaptively organized patterns of interest?

FLIPPING THE VAGAL SWITCH TO REDUCE COGNITIVE INFLEXIBILITY

As outlined in the Introduction, the interventions put forth in this book are designed to create experiences of safety. Autistic nervous systems exist in states of chronic threat but can experience moments of liminal or transitional peace, and in this liminal space we can find moments of calm or ease that parallel a nervous system at rest, one that can, like the mother and son described at the start of Chapter 2, experience a felt sense of safety. It is in these moments that vagal efficiency and recovery speed improve. As outlined in Chapter 2 VAGAL EFFI-CIENCY refers to the ability and speed of a person to return from states of threat, with active sympathetic and dorsal vagal systems (low HRV), to the felt sense of safety associated with the ventral vagal system (high HRV). As the vagal switch gets flipped, that experience of safety begins to grow (Figure 5.1).

This chapter reviews a number of strategies that may elicit these moments of calm and safety, arrived at through physical exhaustion or loss of metabolic energy. With enough flips of the vagal switch, a person with ASD can begin to recognize this sense of safety and learn to be less rigid and restrictive in their patterns of interest and behaviors. The discussion of these strategies—

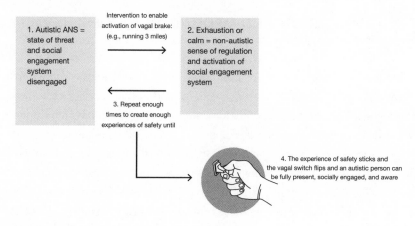

Figure 5.1: Autonomic nervous system
Source: © Sean Inderbitzen via Canva.com

motivational interviewing, increased cardiovascular exercise, and mindful-ness—is folded into descriptions of guiding practices (e.g., neural exercises) related to cognitive inflexibility.

The effectiveness of these strategies would seem to indicate that a person's restrictive and repetitive patterns of thought and behavior are modulated by CARDIO-INHIBITORY PATHWAYS. While this evidence has yet to be deepened by further research, it represents a useful and interesting port of entry into helping our autistic patients become less functionally inhibited by these mal-adaptive ruminations.

NEURAL APPROACHES TO INCREASE COGNITIVE FLEXIBILITY

Neural exercises related to three approaches can reduce cognitive inflexibility. Mindfulness and meditation (several hours per week) reduce ruminations by a statistically significant amount. Cardiovascular exercise increases basal HRV by statistically significant amounts, improving cardiovascular health and resulting in clinically lower amounts of ruminations, with a medium to large effect size. Using basic motivational interviewing in therapy, with emphasis on working with sustained talk, will also help clients work with rumination. Each of these approaches is reviewed below.

PSYCHOEDUCATION AND MEDITATION/MINDFULNESS TO REDUCE RUMINATIONS

Meditation, or the cultivation of awareness for the present moment without judgment, is an ancient practice and has been used in a variety of psychotherapeutic modalities. An important distinction to make as we discuss mindfulness is the difference between cognitive reappraisal and expressive suppression. COGNITIVE REAPPRAISAL is the labeling of an emotional experience and the conscious reformation of the meaning of the situation. For instance, if one partner in a young couple is often flaking, that partner might say, "I would feel mad if I was treated this way" to the other. In contrast, EXPRESSIVE SUPPRESSION aims to hinder the expression of emotions that are not based in the individual's own emotional experience. Expressive suppression often correlates positively with increased symptoms of depression and anxiety (Campbell-Sills et al., 2006). Thus, a key tenet of mindfulness is the cognitive reappraisal of situations with a lack of judgment toward the self.

In the Parmentier et al. (2019) study, a sample of 1,494 participants answered the Mindfulness: Short Five Facets of Mindfulness Questionnaire, Depression and Anxiety: Hospital Depression and Anxiety Scale, Leuven Adaptation of the Rumination on Sadness Scale, Penn State Worry Questionnaire, and Emotion Regulation Questionnaire. Researchers found that "mindfulness decreased depression and anxiety by increasing reappraisal (negatively associated with depression and anxiety) and reducing worry, rumination and suppression (negatively associated with depression and, except for suppression, with anxiety)" (Parmentier et al., 2019). In another set of studies, patients with cancer and depression were able to reduce ruminations and high blood pressure through use of meditation (Campbell et al., 2012; Zainal et al., 2013). A meta-analysis exploring the impact of mindfulness on OCD and PTSD symptoms and parasympathetic activity (Poli et al., 2021) found increased parasympathetic activity, increased vagal tone, and decreased symptoms of PTSD and OCD in patients. These are among the many studies documenting the relationship between mindfulness and reduced rumination and worry.

In a study of 50 autistic adults (Spek et al., 2013), participants went through a nine-week mindfulness-based training and self-evaluated at three intervals. At the end of the study participants showed significantly reduced ratings of ruminations and increased positive affect. Hwang and Kearney (2015) trained six mothers and their autistic children in mindfulness to help them address their own behavioral and psychological challenges. Results reflected positive results for both mothers and children. While more work is needed, these studies suggest that the positive symptom change in reduced rumination reflects an autistic behavior that is malleable with mindfulness through increases in HRV (reduced heart beat speed). Thus, in the Polyvagal Theory–informed neurophysiological model, the trait of rumination indeed correlates with increased activation of the sympathetic and dorsal vagal systems at the cost of decreased activation of the ventral vagus, limiting accessibility to the social engagement system. Thus, the often described symptom of cognitive flexibility, a presumed trait of autism, may be modifiable over time.

Another clinical concern is that autism often is accompanied by the comorbidity dissociation. This comes up frequently for me and for other clinicians I work with who specialize in treating autism and PTSD, primarily in the modalities of EMDR and Sensorimotor Psychotherapy. Per the Mayo Clinic (2017), DISSOCIATION involves "experiencing a disconnection and lack of continuity between thoughts, memories, surroundings, actions and identity. People with dissociative disorders escape reality in ways that are involuntary and unhealthy and cause problems with functioning in everyday life." Dissociation is potentially associated with a dorsal vagal state of collapse: the organism, unable to find a way out of danger, begins to shut down the nervous system, and is immobilized as it is unable to regulate the ventral vagal brake. We can hypothesize based on the animal kingdom how, for some of our ancestors, feigning death or shutting off the pain receptors to the brain may have helped them stay alive on the savannah. But today it presents a concern few have explored in patients with autism: the frequency of dissociative symptoms in autism and how mindfulness might be aptly applied here.

The research literature on this topic is relatively scarce. Five studies have explored the relationship between autism and dissociation, three with youth and two with adults. Zdankiewicz-S'cigała et al. (2021) surveyed 205 adults, 79 of whom were autistic. Those with higher interoceptive scores (i.e., higher awareness of one's internal realities), regardless of ASD diagnosis, had a statistically significantly higher risk of developing a body-based (somatoform) dissociative disorder (Zdankiewicz-S'cigała et al., 2021). This finding suggests an increased risk for body-based dissociative symptoms for those with difficulties with interoception, which is also a well-documented risk factor for those on the autism spectrum.

Reuben and Parish (2021), who surveyed 687 autistic adults using the Multiscale Dissociation Inventory and the Somatoform Dissociation Questionnaire, found 72% of autistic adult respondents endorsed depersonalization, 59% endorsed derealization, 53% observed memory difficulties, and 32% scored at a clinically significant level for a somatoform disorder. The researchers also captured qualitative information to highlight the challenges of those they sampled. One participant (cisgender woman, 22–25 years of age) described it like this:

> I feel that having undiagnosed ASD made me more vulnerable to domestic abuse, which in turn led to dissociative amnesia and identity confusion. Constantly being bamboozled in social situations and trying to adapt myself to fit in has led to identity confusion and alteration. It all ties together—autistic traits lead to me getting into traumatic situations, trying to repress/change who I am, getting confused . . . and the situations are more difficult because I'm autistic. (Reuben & Parish, 2021)

This articulates the challenges to having an autonomic nervous system that is frequently hypoaroused. The danger, for this participant, is "being bamboozled," and results in repression of the self. In short, the ventral brake is no longer regulating.

This research lends credence to the idea that a dampening of the ventral vagal circuit leads to the frequent state of restrictive and repetitive interests, perhaps even to the point of dissociation from both mind and body. Thus, if dissociative symptoms like somatoform disorders, loss of memory, depersonalization, and derealization symptoms are frequently present in autistic individuals, how can they be addressed through mindfulness? Several major types of trauma therapy—including eye movement desensitization and reprocessing (EMDR), Sensorimotor Psychotherapy, and internal family systems therapy—use mindfulness to treat dissociative symptoms.

That said, there is a very limited amount of information on the topic of autism and dissociation, and even less on interventions like mindfulness. Thus, the challenge of dissociation remains a pressing one for clinicians whose autistic clients want to modulate their restrictive, repetitive patterns of thought and behaviors. In a sample of 55 psychiatric patients who reported auditory hallucinations and depersonalization symptoms, Escudero-Pérez et al. (2016) gave the respondents the Mindful Attention Awareness Scale, the Tellegen Absorption Scale, the Cambridge Depersonalization Scale, the Psychotic Symptom Rating Scales, and Positive and Negative Syndrome Scale. They found that distress caused by depersonalization symptoms were most strongly mitigated by mindfulness traits. Though it used a small sample, the study serves as an example of how therapies that employ mindfulness techniques, such as Sensorimotor Psychotherapy (Classen et al., 2021; Jorba Galdos & Warren, 2021), internal family systems therapy (Hodgdon et al., 2022; Pais 2009), and EMDR (van der Hart et al., 2014), might be effective in treating dissociation in its varied forms.

We can learn from these psychotherapy modalities how mindfulness might be integrated in a variety of body-based forms, whether through movement or the use of bilateral stimulation, to engage both hemispheres of the brain. Whatever the pathway, we may need to reimagine how to build mindfulness in a way that encourages the dampened ventral vagal circuit to respond, rather than the disassociation of the dorsal ventral system.

CARDIOVASCULAR EXERCISE TO INCREASE HRV AND LOWER RUMINATIONS

Improved cardiovascular health achieved through increased strenuous cardiovascular exercise will reduce HRV by clinically significant amounts. Statistically significant increases in HRV will result in clinically lower amounts of ruminations with a medium to large effect size.

The evidence about restrictive and repetitive patterns of thought and behavior discussed thus far supports the hypothesis that mindfulness can be an effective intervention to reduce this functionally limiting symptom in autistic persons. From the Polyvagal Theory–informed perspective of autism, cardiovascular inhibitory pathways help form these restrictive and repetitive patterns of behavior and thought. Behaviors associated with autism are not always inherently maladaptive; only when repetitive interests or behaviors become disturbing either to the self or to others can they become maladaptive. The goal of this Polyvagal Theory–informed therapy modality is never to "cure" or mute the identity of an autistic person; rather, *the goal is to modulate the symptoms enough to make these often beautiful adaptations less disturbing* to the individuals and those around them.

Improved cardiovascular health achieved through increased cardiovascular exercise will increase HRV by clinically significant amounts. In keeping with the view that cognitive inflexibility is correlated with lower HRV, evidence suggests that cognitive inflexibility may be a modifiable trait that can be decreased by improving cardiovascular functioning.

Consistent exercise several times per week can achieve a statistically significant change in HRV (Sandercock et al., 2005). In healthy patients, HRV can be modified through aerobic exercise (Dixon et al., 1992; Furlan et al., 1993; Pichot et al., 2005) and does not require a strenuous effort. This exercise must be primarily aerobic to increase cardiovascular health, but patients using this type of intervention experience numerous other benefits as well, including lowered risk in metabolic and cardiovascular diseases (Carnethon et al., 2005; Dixon et al., 1992; Furlan et al., 1993; Kaminsky et al., 2019; Kodama et al., 2009; Lee et al., 2011; Myers et al., 2017; Pichot et al., 2005; Virani et al., 2020).

A fair amount of evidence supports that lower levels of HRV are consistent with maladaptive rumination or perseverations. As previously discussed, in a sample of workers tested for HRV and rumination levels, Cropley et al. (2017) found that the higher the HRV, the lower the incidence of ruminations. Similar results were obtained around the same time by Williams et al. (2017), whose over 200 participants responded to the 22-item RUMINA-TIVE RESPONSES SCALE (RRS) and provided a measure of HRV. They found the same inverse relationship between HRV and ruminations, independently confirming the notion that a cardio-inhibitory mechanism can increase and decrease cognitive flexibility.

HRV can be altered over time with consistent conditioning and exposure to cardio-health-related interventions like HRV biofeedback and nonstrenuous and strenuous levels of exercise. Brand et al. (2018) studied 129 respondents who completed a questionnaire pre/post exercising, and then 30 of these same patients later in the week. In addition to the expected improvements in strength, attention, socialization, and mood, this group of patients, who continued to exercise, showed statistically significant reductions in rumination. Thus, exercise may effectively reduce maladaptive ruminations by decreasing activation of patients' sympathetic and dorsal vagal nervous systems. In a study of a mental and physical training program, Alderman et al. (2016) explored how 52 participants changed in depression and rumination scores over eight weeks. The intervention involved 30 minutes of focused attention and 30 minutes of moderate aerobic exercise. Those with depression ($n = 22$) reported significant decreases in depression and ruminations. These two studies highlight that change in ruminations can occur through aerobic exercise at a moderate level.

There is no research on the direct effectiveness of physical exercise in increasing cognitive flexibility, which in the polyvagal view would follow increased HRV over time with chronic exercise interventions. However, in a meta-analysis of 259 studies on the effectiveness of exercise in ASD, which ultimately selected only 7 for inclusion, owing to strict inclusion criteria, chronic exercise showed statistically significant, small to moderate improvements in executive functioning (Liang et al., 2022), reflecting increased cognitive flexibility.

While not a physical exercise, the Safe and Sound Protocol is a listening exercise tested on autistic children in three studies. Porges et al. (2013) evaluated children with and without autism to analyze changes in RESPIRATORY SINUS ARRHYTHMIA (RSA) and auditory processing performance (SCAN Test for Filtered Words and Competing Words). The intervention significantly enhanced RSA and improved performance on the auditory processing. In the ASD sample, "this pattern of increased RSA during the attention demanding SCAN tests moderated the relation between performance on the Competing Words test and IQ" (Porges et al., 2013). This result lends credence to the idea that improved cognitive performance can be a by-product of increased RSA, whether achieved through the Safe and Sound Protocol or exercise. Two other studies with ASD children (Heilman et al., in press; Porges et al., 2014) further document the positive effect on cognitive performance that auditory interventions can have on children with ASD. Such positive outcomes open the door for therapeutic interventions that incorporate exercise to improve cognitive flexibility.

The effects of altering intensity and duration of exercise still remain a mystery, but the literature is clear that exercise can improve HRV. The exercises must be aerobic: there appears to be a relationship between changes in heart rate and increased mental flexibility. And they must be applied as regularly as possible, to get the most cardio benefit.

Is exercise a reliable cardiac vagal brake? That is, does it reliably enhance the dynamic withdrawal and recovery of the vagal brake, as measured by changes in HRV? A brief review of the literature suggests the answer is yes. Rehabilitating the vagal brake is a lot like building attention through meditation or building muscles by lifting weights. The resistance actually increases strength over time. In a longitudinal study of untrained individuals, six weeks of aerobic exercise reliably reduced resting heart rate (al-Ani et al., 1996). Additionally, multiple studies of athletes (Dannen et al., 2012; Mann et al., 2014), patients with heart failure (Myers et al., 2007; Pearson et al., 2018; Streuber et al., 2006), and patients with type 2 diabetes (Bhati et al., 2018) have demonstrated that resting heart rate can be reliably reduced through exercise. This suggests that neural exercises such as those proposed in this book can also reliably reduce resting heart rate. With a sharp increase in ventral vagal system activity and a significant decrease in sympathetic nervous system activity, we should see increased flexibility through this repeated flipping of the vagal switch.

As Porges (1975) speculated, intentionality of one's attention and actions appears to come more online as parasympathetic activity becomes elevated through the use of exercise and flipping the vagal switch. The ability to sustain attention and bring the executive function system online may be a by-product of applying the vagal brake. Mindfulness exercises can help clients more readily focus on one self-interest in the context of competing self-interests. Thus we can expect clients to be better able to attain their goals, in the context of competing interests, when they feel increasingly regulated (Barkley, 2011; Porges, 1976).

MOTIVATIONAL INTERVIEWING WITH EMPHASIS ON SUSTAINED TALK

MOTIVATIONAL INTERVIEWING (MI) is a counseling method that helps people resolve ambivalent feelings and insecurities to find the internal motivation they need to change their behavior. It is a practical, empathetic, and short-term process that takes into consideration how difficult it is to make life changes (*Psychology Today*, n.d.). The Motivational Interviewing Network of Trainers (MINT, n.d.) notes that MI is

1. based on a respectful and curious way of being with people that facilitates the natural process of change and honors client autonomy;
2. a guiding style of communication that sits between following (good listening) and directing (giving information and advice); and
3. designed to empower people to change by drawing out their own meaning, importance, and capacity for change.

MI was developed to fill a need for more effective ways to treat recovery patients who had experienced dismal outcomes with the traditional Alcoholics Anonymous (AA) model of "turn or burn": if you do not "turn" away from addictive behaviors, you are certain to encounter dire consequences ("burn"). The

MI approach, in contrast, is rooted in the belief that change is brought about through meaningful engagement and partnership with clients' expertise on their own lives.

Currently, little evidence supports the effectiveness of MI with autistic adults or children, nor is it widely taught. I run one of the few trainings available for using MI with autistic adults. During trainings, which I give for clinicians, social workers, and nurses, I often show a video called *It's Not About the Nail* to demonstrate the "righting" reflex. In this video a woman is complaining to a man about an aching, throbbing sensation in her skull. As the camera pans out we see a giant nail in her head. This nail is the first thing the man comments on, and the woman replies, "You're doing it again. It's not about the nail." She then proceeds to tell him what she needs is not for him to fix it but for him to just give her space to express herself about the nail. As he does this, she then appreciates the lack of response he gives. I show this amusing video to highlight how we all tend to try to "fix" things rather than just hold space for the pain. I would argue it is more beneficial to our clients to give them this space than to try to resolve the pain. It is also a harder task—we must fight against the natural human longing to resolve the pain of those we love or serve.

Research demonstrates again and again, across a wide range of disciplines, that MI helps people make change through partnership rather than through directiveness. A central way of thinking about this practice, when working with patients on the spectrum, is that we should try to "dance" with them: follow their lead rather than trying to lead or admonish them. The word "dance" describes so well the back and forth between patient and client working together to drive meaningful change. It is achieved not by demanding or by healing but, rather, as Ron Kurtz (2009; as cited in Ogden, 2021) so eloquently notes in the epigraph to Chapter 2.

CLINICAL IMPLICATIONS

Neural exercises work with clients on ruminations—restrictive, repetitive patterns of behaviors and thoughts—via motivational interviewing, increased cardiovascular exercises, and mindfulness. The central aim of visceromotor psychotherapy is to help clients on the spectrum modulate the trait of rumination to be less functionally impairing in their life course, so they might achieve the cognitive flexibility they so desire. One could say the goal is "to be less autistic," but what I've described is simply expanding the ability to be more flexible and able to adapt to changes that fall outside of one's chosen patterns whose restrictive, repetitive nature interferes with quality of life.

The intention is never to "cure" the autism but, rather, to guide the autonomic nervous system away from a chronic state of threat, into an easier place that has benefits, including improved cardiovascular health and improved emotional and cognitive flexibility. People with cognitive inflexibility can learn to be more aware of their own internal somatic, emotional, and cognitive states, by integrating themselves into the present moment and better understanding their own desires and challenges, through motivational interviewing, mindfulness, and increased cardiovascular exercises. Chapters 6 and 7 offer techniques for mindfulness and cardiovascular exercises that can be incorporated into practice. Chapter 8 offers more discussion of motivational interviewing, in the context of building social communication skills, and includes recommendations for further reading. These brief descriptions only touch the surface of the much deeper practice of motivational interviewing—clinicians should have at least basic training in this technique before employing it in their practice.

CHAPTER 6

Mindfulness Exercises

You must love in such a way that the person you love feels free.

THICH NHAT HANH

Applying mindfulness is an ongoing process and takes some space for learning. Getting into a mindful state from a chronic state of threat is no easy task, whether you are trying to do this for yourself, for someone you love, or for a client. This chapter addresses some of the common challenges and strategies that work. These are by no means an exhaustive list of mindfulness-based strategies. They are derived from personal and clinical experience with people with autism. The process of applying mindfulness can be thought of as a three-step process: (1) learn about mindfulness, (2) find the right intensity of mindfulness, and (3) engage in mindfulness.

Note that mindfulness is being applied here to address cognitive inflexibility, or what is more commonly called restrictive, repetitive interests. Such restrictive interests or obsessions are self-reinforcing by nature. At some point we began telling ourselves a story that had some adaptive and soothing elements. As we repeat these stories again and again, they become less adaptive and more disruptive to relationships or activities. The stories we tell ourselves take root, until the messages they send us no longer match what is actually happening in the present. As we begin our journey on the path of mindfulness, we need to cultivate awareness of the stories that keep taking us away from the present. They might be soothing or self-reinforcing, but the present has so much more to offer than these restrictive, repetitive interests.

Neural Exercise: Mindfulness as a Strategy

Mindfulness is a lot like coffee: its strength and desired intensity may vary from person to person. "Intensity," much like the term suggests, is related to the quality or force applied to something. In the context of this book, INTENSITY refers to the level of silence a meditation practice introduces to a listener. The more intense the strategy, the more silence within the meditation. For clinicians, meditation is perhaps one of the hardest skills to integrate into practice, because of its perceived metabolic cost, a cost in terms of energy that is more witnessed than researched at this point but takes a toll on overall energy level. We have witnessed the cost in energy for our autistic clients to engage in dual awareness (awareness of both the present moment and past experiences), so it is best to begin slowly. It may be helpful to think of mindfulness not as stillness but as *present-moment awareness*. Mindfulness can occur when an adult is cooking or fishing or when a child is bouncing on a ball. Such awareness can be baked into nearly any activity, as long as the intensity matches the ability and tolerance of the individual.

Mindfulness may be introduced through psychoeducation, and your method will depend on the demographics of your clients. For young clients, video games, especially virtual reality, can be a wonderful pathway by which to introduce mindfulness in a slow and tolerable way. There are some research-based mindfulness applications, such as the game *VR Tripp*, used to calm the autonomic nervous systems of high-performance athletes. If a client's special interest involves video games, this can be a way to introduce mindfulness that is connected to an existing repetitive interest. The function of repetitive interests can be thought of as self-soothing, so if video games or tablet time is a restrictive, repetitive behavior, mindfulness through this pathway can be seen as a self-soothing tool that also helps develop a vital skill.

The ethics of reinforcing a restrictive, repetitive interest or behavior depends on how maladaptive that may be, a question that can only be answered in the context of the therapeutic space and cannot be prescribed per se. In keeping with the value of GENEROSITY, the client and family are the experts on their own lives, in this as in other matters. Thus, the ethics of this decision is informed by the individual family context within which it occurs.

Other strategies include mindfulness directives, mindfulness questions, and contact statements (Ogden et al., 2006; Ogden & Fisher, 2015; Ogden et al., 2021). Along with matching of intervention intensity to client ability as you introduce mindfulness, an appropriate level of COGNITIVE SCAFFOLDING is needed. Cognitive scaffolding (sometimes referred to as the zone of proximal development) refers to the amount and type of support a client needs to get from what Lev Vygotsky would have referred to as a student's inability to be where we want them to be. So in the case of mindfulness what types of modifications to the mindfulness are needed, these could be things like finding a faster-paced mindfulness, a shorter mindfulness, a beginner's mindfulness, one that has fewer words, all of which are client dependent to match to the zone of proximal development. When approaching mindfulness with a hyperaroused nervous system in an autistic individual, perhaps the place to start is with a set of a mindfulness directives, a strategy used when the most scaffolding is needed, to promote mindful awareness around a directed behavior. The magic in mindfulness is what happens in a person's mind, not necessarily what they state out loud.

A BODY SCAN is a mindfulness directive to explore various parts of the body, with little to no guidance on the part of the therapist. In using this body scan technique, you may wish to start with attention at the top of the body and to work down. You can also provide directed attention toward various parts of the body or an object of focus, with mindfulness directives that connect a sensation, emotion, or thought to an object or body part, such as, "Tell me about what you are experiencing in that place in your body where you feel the tension."

If the autistic client needs less direction and can already engage in reflective practice, mindfulness questions are a useful strategy. These are questions that evoke dual awareness and lead the client to notice the present-moment experience. Questions often sound open-ended and somewhat open to interpretation, for example, "What do you notice when . . ." or "Can you notice how that lands in your body?" The goal here is internal reflection, not dialogue. Depending on the client's level of cognitive impairment, the therapist may or may not be able to cultivate mindful curiosity in such an open-ended way. For those with less cognitive capacity, or younger minds, questions like, "Could you repeat that? I didn't catch it," are great mindfulness questions; they force the speaker to slow down and become mindful of how fast or slow they are speaking. If they repeat it quickly, the therapist can merely restate the question and ask that the client slow down, and then mindfully explore what it is like to go slower.

With these strategies, the therapist can use the therapeutic space to cultivate awareness in the client around their own restrictive and repetitive patterns of thought and behavior. Often, in pursuit of the self-soothing these patterns provide, the autistic person can overwhelm the listening party with how repetitively they offer the same information on a certain topic of interest. In some cases there is not an off switch, due to their inefficient vagal regulation. The challenging task of therapy, then, becomes helping the autistic person notice when they are or are not caught in the loop of a restrictive, repetitive pattern of thought or behavior. The shorthand for this is *noticing ruminations*; applying mindfulness to this noticing cultivates social awareness.

The therapy space is not only a place to apply mindfulness but also a space to practice meditation, depending on the comfort level of the client. Many mindfulness applications, such as Headspace, allow modifying the voice of the speaker (male/female), level of loudness, length of time (e.g., 3 or 5 min), and the amount of silence (e.g., beginner vs. intermediate), which is perhaps the hardest thing to modulate. One way to assign this practice as homework is to have the autistic individual find a focus for meditation surrounding a restrictive, repetitive interest, thus making the practice soothing while cultivating of awareness, for example, watching a mindfulness video on Pokémon for a client who loves Pokémon.

In terms of modifying existing therapeutic approaches, there are some parallels to what is called acceptance and commitment therapy (ACT), created by Steven Hayes. Developed in the 1980s, it uses key skills of mindfulness and acceptance to transform an individual's response to a situation (Hayes, n.d.). Hayes's work with ACT is highly compatible with the techniques described in this chapter that apply mindfulness to help clients reach states of safety. There is also significant acceptance in the field of applied behavioral analysis (ABA) for the use of ACT, which relies on behavioral sciences. If you use ACT as a strategy, you will need to measure and match for pace (how much slowness a client with autism can successfully tolerate) and intensity (how much silence the client can endure) based on prior exposure.

When I interviewed Steven Hayes for this book, we had a dynamic conversation. At one point I asked him, "What do you make of applied behavioral analysis in its present state?" He replied,

I think of myself as a behavioral analyst but not in the traditional sense, relying solely on learning principles from nonhuman animals. I departed from that wing about 35 years ago or so, but applied behavioral analysis was born in trying to serve the downtrodden, the poor and cognitively delayed—people who no one else would have helped. I'm old enough to remember people with cognitive delays being housed in concrete rooms in institutions where they would be hosed down. Behavioral analysis was the only discipline interested in treating these individuals with compassion and faith in their ability to progress. Some of that positive history has gotten lost in recent years. The science and practice needs to move forward. (S. Hayes, personal communication, June 8, 2023)

What he said reminded me of what a professor of mine, Dr. Bruce Thyer from Tulane School of Social Work, once said: "If you want to go into nearly anything, get a master's in social work, if you want to really help people get a degree in behavioral analysis" (B. Thyer, personal communication, February 14, 2021). Behavioral analysis, despite how it is commonly characterized by opponents, has beautiful roots in a space that values the complexity of the inner life of the human being. ACT, which is a third wave cognitive behavioral therapy, concerns itself with understanding and knowing what drives a person, and using that understanding to help them.

MEASURING MINDFULNESS

Many applications related to mindfulness are best measured in terms of minutes spent on mindfulness between sessions. Most contain a counting metric to facilitate setting practice times between sessions. The consistent use of a chosen strategy, over and over again, rather than the engagement of one long session of silence, changes behavior and thought patterns. There are several good tools to measure changes in the client's level of rumination. For autistic adults, a great tool is the ADULT REPETITIVE BEHAVIOR QUESTIONNAIRE-2 (ARBQ-2), a self-report measure that presumes a certain level of cognitive ability. Barrett et al. (2018) assessed its reliability in a sample of 275 autistic adults (4 excluded, 100 males, 171 females) and found it both valid and reliable using Cronbach's alpha and correlational analysis. The ARBQ-2, while designed as a self-report measure, can be used for pre/post testing to show change over time. While it is a great tool for measurement of restrictive and repetitive patterns of behavior, it does not capture clinical nuances clinicians may use to show change in cognitive flexibility, or a shift in repetitive interests. Perhaps the most widely used tool to measure changes in interests or rigid thinking patterns is the 8-item RUMINATIVE RESPONSE SCALE (RRS) (Treynor et al., 2003). Williams et al. (2021) asked a cross-sample of 608 autistic adults to complete the RRS and the Beck Depression Index 2, which has a rumination index and found a strong positive correlation between the two measures, which supports the perceived validity of the RRS for both autistic and nonautistic adults. A pre/post testing approach could show if change is being achieved or not, but this tool can be used several times during treatment to show a client's change over time—the more data available to the clinician, the more accurate the treatment results are likely to be.

Measuring changes in autistic youth has an added challenge: ensuring reliability of a treatment in a developing brain that does not have fully developed executive function, and perhaps even developmental delays. Parent-report measures are included to address this measurement problem.

The Social Impact of Repetitive Behaviors Scale (Grossi et al., 2021) demonstrates both good reliability and retest validity as a parent measure for reporting on changes in the social impact of repetitive patterns in autistic youth between infancy and 12 years of age. This tool measures behaviors like repetitive behaviors (e.g., hand flapping and body rocking), self-injurious behaviors, compulsive behaviors, ritualized behaviors, and insistence on sameness. The instrument had excellent interrater reliability ($p < 0.001$), test-retest validity (t-test, 95%), and internal consistency (Cronbach's alpha $= 0.98$). Given its high validity and reliance on social impact and well-being, the Social Impact of Repetitive Behaviors Scale can be considered a gold standard for measurement in clinical practice.

Self-report measures for autistic youth should be applied sparingly. We lack a fully developed theoretical understanding about how self-perception impacts autistic youth's experiences. However, in keeping with the spirit of the neural exercises in this book, autistic youth can be perceived as experts on themselves, despite their known limitations in self-perception. Client expertise is applied in concert with clinician and parental expertise. The therapist must select a measure for treatment that adequately reflects the available sets of expertise. The tool recommended here may not be sufficient to capture changes experienced by an autistic youth but can be used to measure changes in symptoms. The Survey of Favorite Interests and Activities yields no psychometrically valid composite score, as was hoped by researchers, but does have relatively useful independent subscales, like the perseveration scale (Nevill et al., 2020), and can be added as a way to incorporate more of a young autistic client's voice in the measurement treatment outcomes. Autistic self-advocates frequently state concern that children and teens with autism are quite stifled in their opinions about treatment. Including the perseveration scale is a means to involve young clients in their own treatment plans.

Case Example: Beck

Beck was a 35-year-old female with a promising job as a marketing executive at a Fortune 500 company who had been married to her husband, Dutch, for two years. She had been given a diagnosis of autism and attention-deficit/hyperactivity disorder and came to see me for struggles related to her marriage. She shared that Dutch wants to keep trying for a baby and that she fights him intensely, which often leads to him complaining that he feels overwhelmed and needs space. In their most recent conflict, he said it might be best for them to separate, considering how little she was able to recognize when he had had enough.

Beck sat in my office, staring at me blankly, and said, "I just want to be there for him, but I get so invested. It's like I can't stop and he just gives up." "Does he?" I replied. She looked at me and said tentatively, "Maybe?" "How has that worked so far?" "Not well," she replied. "So what if we try something new, related to what we can control . . . you." She looked up.

"Have you heard of mindfulness before?" I asked. "Isn't that where you sit and go ohhmm?" she asked. "No," I replied. "Can I share a video with you?" "Sure, go for it."

I then cued a meditation 101 video (Davis, 2015) on my computer, and she watched fully, smiling as he discussed the process of trying, failing, and trying again. After the video, she looked at me and said, "So how does this help me fight better?" "Well," I replied, "It's about becoming more flexible and beginning to notice when you are getting stuck . . ." "Kind of like, when I avoid my husband because I get too stuck in my frustration?" "Yes," I replied. "So how do we start?" she asked eagerly.

"Why don't we try this meditation app, Headspace," I said. Not thinking, I picked the first meditation that came up, an advanced module. I hit the play button and the voice spoke: "Hi. Welcome to Headspace. I'm Andy. Get comfy and relax. I'll check in with you in a little bit." Roughly two minutes passed, full silence from Andy. Beck had checked out from the meditation and was busy counting the light blotches on the ceiling. Noticing this, I paused the meditation and asked, "So how is this working for you?" Beck in her wisdom responded, "Not great. I have a hard time focusing with all the silence." I looked at her and said softly, "My apologies. Why don't we try one that is a little more engaging?" Being more mindful myself this time, I looked for a beginner's module, with a long introduction and very short periods of silence, the speaker staying with the listener for almost the entire episode.

At the end of the five minutes, Beck said, "That made more sense." "I thought so," I replied. "It helps when I'm mindful as well, not just you." She grinned. "So if you are open to it," I continued, "can I share what I'm thinking might work?" She responded, "Go for it." With her permission I suggested, "Download Headspace, and try doing the beginner series at three- or five-minute intervals, at least four of the next seven days, until I see you next." "Okay," she said, and off she went. Two weeks later Beck returned to my office having well exceeded my expectations. She reported she was meditating almost daily, and as a result, she was finding she was better able to tolerate the uncertainty of the conflict with her husband and to give him space when she sensed herself becoming elevated.

Presenting Problem

At first glance it would be easy to assume that the sole problem to be addressed with Beck was cognitive inflexibility, given the title of the chapter, and Beck's report of her lack of willingness to engage with her husband. However, looking at this rigidly often misses the rest of the diagnostic portrait. In Beck's case we know she has attention-deficit/hyperactivity disorder, characterized by inattention. Thus, we must address not only the cognitive rigidity but also the inattention, which may or may not be super obvious, depending on Beck's presentation.

Intervention

As noted above, mindfulness as an intervention is a three step process: learn about it, find the right intensity, and engage. The introduction to mediation I use in my practice (Davis, 2015) describes mindfulness as (1) trying to clear your mind, (2) getting distracted, and (3) starting again. This process of failure and reattempt is quite successful: by expecting to fail, one engages in the process without self-judgment. What makes this difficult for Beck is her overactive nervous system, which is locked in a state of threat. The lessening of distractibility, an incredibly common problem, is perhaps the most stretching part of this practice for her.

Psychoeducation can be a relatively simple process. You can use YouTube videos or a social story for demonstration, provided clients have the attentional span to engage and do not have severe communication impairments. SOCIAL STORIES according to their creator, Carol Gray, "are a social learning tool that supports the safe and meaningful exchange of information between parents, professionals, and people with autism of all ages" (Gray, 2015). The complexities of trying to focus on clearing one's mind, failing, and repeating, over and over again, may need to be taught with one-to-one instruction, which can be delivered either at a later date or by a paraprofessional who can translate the processes involved in mindfulness for the client.

Mindfulness is largely a bidirectional strategy, intended as much to be modeled by the therapist as used by the client. With Beck we see me not being mindful and, as a result, leading Beck to what could have been the very end of the intervention, were she not so forgiving. Being mindful is, to the highly distractible mind, a radical act that breaks a lifetime of survival strategies. For autistic persons, not being present is a way to cope with being in a world that is frequently distressing. Whether that distress comes from perceived threat, loud noises, bright fluorescent lights, or something else, the autistic mind has become accustomed to not being fully in the present moment. Under these circumstances, engaging in one's feelings or participating in reciprocal social interaction is highly challenging. Thus, it is important to match the level of intensity as well as possible with the client's level of ability to be present.

As Beck's example shows, for a client's first time engaging in mindfulness-based exercises, it's usually best to begin with a meditation that is not complete silence. If we think about the autistic self as being in relationship to the strategy of meditation, it's important to not overload the relationship on the front end. Consider that your nervous system might feel overloaded if you begin with even 5–10 minutes of complete silence. What is nice about starting with the help of an app is that they often have a variety of options to select from, to tailor the length of the medication, the amount of silence, and so on.

For instance, one might consider starting with a beginner course totaling only three minutes. While this might feel inadequate, the goal is not to do this just once but to build a new pattern of practice—starting off easy is a highly purposeful way to begin, so that a client's nervous system can handle the amount of silence being introduced. For more experienced users there are more advanced courses on these apps that have varying durations. The dosing is really based on the therapist's clinical judgment about how much silence a client can tolerate. More is not necessarily better—practicing with short bursts builds and deepens the client's ability to tolerate uncertainty within the client's present capabilities.

Remember that meditation is a radical act for the autistic nervous system—not reinforcing whatever pattern of thought or behavior they are targeting is going to be a new experience. If you or the client responds with frustration or a screeching utterance, this will only deepen that repetitive interest and prevent the adoption of a mindful posture of curiosity and observation, rather than self-judgment.

CLINICAL IMPLICATIONS

Whether you are yourself a person on the spectrum, or the parent, therapist, or teacher of someone who is, mindfulness has numerous benefits for modifying cognitive inflexibility. Whether by sitting and meditating or by moving and bouncing on a yoga ball, achieving mindful awareness is one path to teach the nervous system how to regulate and enter the social engagement system. Through meditating, the autistic person is breaking a lifetime habit of chronic threat state. And our own nervous system, which we as therapists bring into the room, affects our ability to establish this type of disruptive experience for our clients.

CHAPTER 7

Cardiovascular Exercises

....

The most deadly disease truly is the failure of the heart.
                                        OSCAR ARIAS

APPLYING EXERCISE AND BIOFEEDBACK

The average life expectancy of a person with autism, without intellectual disabilities, is 58 years, and for those with severe autism it is only 39.5 years (Heiss et al., 2021; Sala et al., 2020); compare this with the average overall life span of individuals in the United States (78.8 years), in the United Kingdom (81.2 years), and in India (69.66 years). Thus, having autism alone is a significant predictor of shorter life expectancy in nearly any modernized country. From a body lens or sensorimotor lens, autism is consistent with a much higher resting heart rate and lower heart rate variability (HRV). Rosenthal et al. (2021) looked at the genetic networks of 2,628 people; the networks for those with autism ($n = 27$) and those with congenital heart failure ($n = 46$) shared 7 common genes. This is significant in and of the fact that from a PVT model of autism lens, genetic and environmental factors give rise to the behavioral phenotype seen symptomatically, and Rosenthal et al. (2021) point to a genetic link.

Thus, autism, while primarily thought of as a disorder of neurodevelopment, in fact also has physiological effects. The body of an autistic person is part of what gives rise to this specific constellation of behaviors of cognitive inflexibility and social communication deficits. It is a disordering not just of development of the human mind but also of one's vagal efficiency. Learning to activate the vagal brake is a skill that does not come naturally to those on the spectrum—it takes neural exercises to flip the vagal switch to become more flexible. The vagal switch flipping interventions suggested here, from the domains of exercise and biofeedback, outline a set of ways to help persons with autism begin to build that vagal brake and regulate some of the cognitive rigidity that comes with feeling unsafe and threatened.

EXERCISES TO INCREASE HEART RATE VARIABILITY

Given the link between HRV and autism, therapists must work with our autistic patients to improve their physical health, as a means both of improving life expectancy and of reducing cognitive inflexibility by raising HRV. Traditional psychotherapy is associated with cognitive processing; increasing HRV is far more behavioral than cognitive. Cognitive strategies might be used in motivational interviewing to overcome barriers to exercising, but the goals are primarily related to the centrality of increasing HRV.

To review briefly: HEART RATE refers to the number of heart beats per minute. HEART RATE VARIABILITY (HRV), in contrast, is the *variation* in time between adjacent heart beats. Low HRV—similar times between beats even with a change in environment—can be thought of as not healthy, whereas higher HRV, allowing greater variation in timing to fit the circumstances, can be thought of as healthier. All humankind lives on a continuum of HRV health, and those with autism are statistically at the lower end (Patriquin et al., 2019). So except for clients who are highly athletic, chances are that an autistic person will benefit from improving this facet of physical and psychological health. The desired end result is modulation of cognitive inflexibility to the point that it is less socially damaging.

As discussed in Chapter 5, there is a CARDIO-INHIBITORY PATHWAY that leads to activation of the sympathetic nervous system and dorsal vagal system. Cognitive rigidity can be thought of as an expression of routine activation of these threat states. Thus, the strategy of introducing cardiovascular exercise in a way that elevates HRV could directly modify cognitive flexibility.

While a variety of factors appear to be linked to changes in HRV, the primary approach for this Polyvagal Theory–informed modality is increased activation of this cardiac link through exercise. The exercise does not need to be overly strenuous; simple aerobic exercise multiple times per week is sufficient (Sandercock et al., 2005). This exercise can be variable in duration, length, intensity, and frequency, based on the needs of the individual's autonomic nervous system. Again, the goal is never to "cure" autism; rather, it is to modify the rigidity to the point that the client can function socially at a level they desire. The client is the expert on their desired level of change, and practical quantitative measures in combination with the qualitative nature of self-report are the way to guide therapy to achieve the desired change.

MEASURING HEART RATE VARIABILITY

Because, in general, lower HRV is less healthy and higher HRV healthier, HRV has become a common metric in exercise, physiology, and human performance psychology. The challenge is that HRV, like many other scientific constructs, is not easily isolated or interpreted. For instance, those with eating disorders tend to violate this general pattern. Heiss et al. (2021) found that those with anorexia nervosa and bulimia tend to demonstrate higher HRV. Fasting may be associated with changes in HRV, and may account for this effect.

While no ideal rates of HRV are recommended here, the existing literature supports an impetus toward increasing HRV to a higher range. This is especially true for persons with autism, who may be at the lower end of the HRV continuum. However, the therapist may consider eating patterns when trying to influence a client's level of cognitive flexibility, particularly if the client has difficulty in changing their level of HRV.

A variety of metrics are potentially useful for measuring HRV. For therapeutic work here we consider short-term HRV, with a focus on respiratory sinus arrhythmia (RSA) (Porges, 2022), an existing and valid measurement in autistic children. Since RSA is primarily measured in medical settings with an echocardiogram, you may consider working with the patient's local clinic system to obtain pre/post measurements. A number of commercially available devices can measure RSA, but no devices or apps are specific enough for reimbursers to consider reliable. The recommendation here is to use dual metrics: a combination of a biofeedback metric (e.g., an echocardiogram) and psychometric feedback (e.g., the Ruminative Response Scale for autistic adults, the Social Impact of Repetitive Behaviors Scale, or the Survey of Favorite Interests and Activities). Pairing biometric measures of RSA with psychometric measures of repetitive interests offers our clients a fuller view of themselves and their progress toward their goals.

For a more full discussion of HRV measurement instruments it is recommended to reach out to the Kinsey Institute Traumatic Stress Research Consortium, which regularly contracts with government agencies to conduct studies on HRV. Frequently among their selected instruments for measuring HRV before and after a sit-to-stand exercise, Kinsey uses the Muse 2 headset, which is commercially available. While it is not the only instrument to measure HRV, this can be done in conjunction with a wearable EEG and ECG sensor called the Firstbeat Bodyguard 2. Bodyguard and Muse 2 provide a much more accurate reading of HRV that is statistically reliable as compared to something like the Apple Watch, which does not have an accurate enough measurement system to capture the changes in HRV discussed in this book.

Neural Exercise: Biofeedback to Increase HRV

Although modifying an individual's cardiac health ties to improvements in cognitive rigidity, therapists and clients alike may not like exercise and may even find the idea repulsive. Let me reassure you that nobody is asking clients to do anything that is very physically strenuous. Running nearly 10 miles per week year-round has become my personal habit to deal with my own rigidity. That said, in no way is the expectation for you or your clients to run even a mile. Here, a certain level and repetition of physical exercise is a tool for bringing the vagal brake online—a way to practice flipping the vagal switch.

One of the key features that distinguish autism from obsessive-compulsive disorder is that the repetitive interests of an autistic individual are self-soothing. They allow the individual to enter into a mental state that is similar to what positive psychology refers to as "flow" or as a state of being "in the zone." This is a mental state reached when an individual is completely immersed, present, and enjoying the performance of some task (Ellis et al., 1994; Csíkszentmihályi, n.d.). With OCD, a person's repetitive thoughts are often intrusive and unwanted, whereas with autism, as with someone in a state of flow, these repetitive interests are welcomed. The challenge is that returning to these soothing thoughts or behaviors can become a habit that is hard to shake, and their persistence often works to the detriment of interpersonal relationships.

Case Example: Joseph

Joseph, a 35-year-old male, lived with his parents and a sister. He came in presenting with concerns of what he termed "mad mares," where he would wake up midway through sleep screaming. His step-mother described the process of being available for him a bit like wearing kid-friendly gloves.

However, Joseph expressed sympathy for his father, stepmother, and sister and wanted to be able to be more flexible in life. He reported to me one day, "I'm tired of people having to tiptoe around me as if I'm going to explode." "Well that's insightful," I said, rather stunned and unaware that he had this much capacity. Laughing, Joseph looked at me and said, "My brain gets really sticky when people change things about me. It's a bit like chewing gum. I'd like my brain to be a little less sticky." "That might be possible," I replied, "but you would have to work at it." "Anything," Joseph replied.

With that Joseph and I brainstormed ways he might engage in physical exercises, and he landed on doing planks. The plan was for him to do planks or, as he termed it, resistance exercises when he felt himself getting angry. That week he went home and tried it. When he returned next week, he said, "Strangely that worked." "What do you mean?" I asked. "Well, my sister decided we needed to go back to Spooner [their hometown] for something for her job, and this really caught me off guard. I felt my fists getting tighter and my chest tightening, and so I removed myself and did some. After five minutes I was ready to go, and no more anger." "Weird," I replied. "Almost like we planned this or something."

Presenting Problem

While Joseph had a series of presenting challenges, his greatest barrier was his rigidity, not his mad mares. While these were challenging, and presented first, they were not what Joseph ultimately was concerned with. As we got to know each other, it became clear that he wanted to be less rigid and more flexible (note his apt description of a "chewing gum" brain). It helped that one of Joseph's repetitive interests was exercising, which made engaging in exercise an easy form of intervention to undertake.

Intervention

Therapists can encounter significant potential barriers to getting a client with autism to engage with exercise. Using a person's repetitive interest to engage them in heart-rate-increasing exercise is a great avenue to modify this cardiac link. One example of a nonstrenuous exercise intervention is the use of the popular phone-based game, Pokémon Go. In this game, players walk around various geographic locations trying to find and catch a digital Pokémon linked to their actions through a real-world mapping program. For a client obsessed with Pokémon, this game is an example of an activity that might engage them in exercise in a self-soothing way.

The goal is not to trick anyone, however, but to motivate them to motivate themselves to exercise. It will help clients to understand that by engaging in exercise, they can expect the persistence of their repetitive thoughts to decrease and their cognitive flexibility to increase. In short we are getting them to flip that vagal switch, again and again building with it new strength each time that vagal switch is flipped.

As such, engaging with interest-based activities that include exercise is a great strategy, for at least two reasons. It builds both a connection between a restrictive pattern while increasing mental flexibility. Joseph's love of exercises and use of planks, for example, was not an intervention I as the clinician brought to the table but one he already knew. In keeping with the values of ORGANICITY and RESPECT, we let Joseph's inner wisdom guide us to that solution. While exercise is a research-based intervention, it was the blending of this expertise with Joseph's own inner wisdom that allowed us to arrive at an intervention he actually adopted. Interestingly, he eventually practiced this enough to go on a trip with his niece and nephew; he could remove himself anytime they annoyed him and exercise to reduce his rigidity toward them.

CLINICAL IMPLICATIONS

Exercise or movement that is strenuous enough to raise a person's heart rate is really all it takes to train the nervous system to begin to come out of states of threat. This intervention need not be all-consuming and can be used in both individual and group settings, whether one on one in an outpatient setting or one on seven in a day treatment or hospitalization program. The goal is to increase HRV to allow for increased mental flexibility. In short, we can use exercise to flip the vagal switch, with the immediate benefit of giving clients new space to make decisions when stressed.

While the body may seem a strange place to begin, for more top-down approach practitioners (e.g., those who practice primarily EMDR, dialectical behavioral therapy, or cognitive behavioral therapy), the human body is indeed a place where therapy occurs. While often forgotten, it is always physically present, perhaps unconsciously, in ways that more traditional approaches might not acknowledge. This is important to reflect on, because some practitioners refer to autism as a disorder of delayed motor control. The physical body is often overlooked in our rational, brain-based culture—to borrow a general concept from Daniel Siegel, humans have a number of brains, or independent neural processing networks; by brains we mean to use the metaphor that our body parts all together give rise to consciousness (Siegel, 1999) not just a head brain but also a gut brain, a heart brain, a stomach brain, and so on. Our body is fully present any time we do the work of psychotherapy, and it deserves greater consideration than traditionally given, if we really want to see meaningful change in the realm of cognitive flexibility.

PART 3

Polyvagal Theory–Informed Interventions for Social Communication

CHAPTER 8

Addressing Social Communication

∙∙

When you've met one person with autism, you've met one person with autism.

DR. STEPHEN SHORE, *"AMBITIOUS ABOUT AUTISM"*

This quote captures a broader theme relevant to autism and beyond. Human beings all have their own beautiful, at times confusing, and maybe even horrible idiosyncrasies. In short, no two people are alike. Relying on this diversity of cognitive style, and neurological presentation, appears at face value to be a great strategy for normalizing seemingly strange behaviors. Yet very little medical science over the last 30 years supports the existence of differential neuroanatomy or neurophysiology in people with autism. But what we can say with relative confidence, to support the neurodiversity hypothesis, is that they differ in nervous system state. People with autism exist in a rather enduring state of fight/flight or collapse and have difficulty feeling safe. This difference gives rise to demonstrably differential thought patterns and behaviors that might be conceptualized as adaptive and maladaptive strategies of the autistic self. Much as in traumatized individuals, these strategies can be thought of as doing their best to prevent threats from impacting the autistic person's nervous system but are also causing them distress. It becomes the key task of therapy to increase sociability by making clients feel safe. Safety, not demand, is what will lead to change.

FLIPPING THE VAGAL SWITCH FOR SOCIAL ENGAGEMENT

As noted throughout this book, the repeated use of interventions can lead the autonomic nervous system of an autistic person out of a chronic state of threat (see Figure 8.1). Through interventions the vagal switch gets flipped repeatedly, enabling the social engagement states/ventral vagal states to come online, creating flexibility and openness, often a root goal for autistic clients who want to go with the flow of daily life. The repeated switching of the vagal switch eventually shapes the space needed to turn on the social gears of the autistic brain. Only in this liminal space of the ventral vagal system can people with autism become aware of social cues that are not perceived as threats. Turning off this state of threat, using the interventions outlined in Part 2, can help engage and release the vagal brake enough to begin using the interventions described here in Part 3. Treatment is far from a linear process, but in these brief yet more enduring moments when clients experience safety, interventions to improve social engagement can help bring change. Only when a person with ASD is in a ventral vagal state can we begin to apply these social interventions and, over time, widen that awareness until, ideally, achieving a more *reliable state of safety.*

Chapter 1 described a father holding his infant son—the child felt securely attached and hence the crying stopped, and there was a shared gaze. With the intervening chapters you have read, my hope is that this story now resonates with deeper meaning. When people with autism are in a ventral vagal state, they carry a sense of safety and can begin to look more like that father and child, who are not neurologically in a state of threat. They can make eye contact, be flexible, read their own feeling states, and engage in reciprocal communication. To cultivate these capabilities is the overarching goal of therapy: to move the autistic person from their rather rigid and unmoving state to a more flexible, grounded, and mindful state. Flipping the vagal switch repeatedly has the potential to help our autistic clients learn to reach this chronic ventral vagal state.

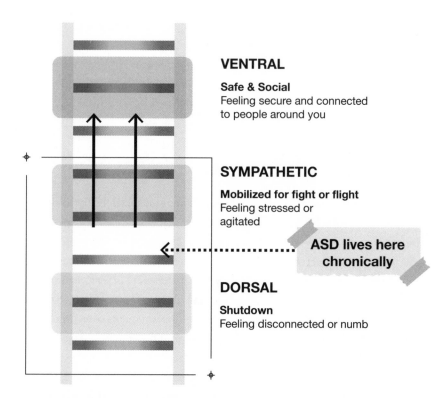

Figure 8.1: Autistic nervous systems alternate between fight/flight and freeze/ collapse (boxed area). The goal of therapy is to help the nervous system experience safety (solid arrows), so clients can learn to flip the vagal switch on their own. Source: Adapted from POLYVAGAL FLIP CHART: UNDERSTANDING THE SCIENCE OF SAFETY by Deb Dana. Copyright © 2020 by Deborah A. Dana. Used by permission of W. W. Norton & Company, Inc.

NEURAL EXERCISES FOR SOCIAL ENGAGEMENT

You may recall that in Chapter 5 the three neural approaches to reduce cognitive inflexibility: mindfulness/meditation, cardio exercises, and motivational interviewing. This chapter explores two additional approaches related to the cultivation of safety:

Increasing a sense of safety, through skills building and practice, psychoeducation, and somatic and other resources (e.g., deep

breathing and hand over heart), will result in significantly higher
heart rate variability (HRV) at the clinical level.

Building social communication skills, using approaches from social
work and/or clinical psychology pedagogy, which can improve
these skills by a statistically significant level.

INCREASING A SENSE OF SAFETY

Coping strategies from Sensorimotor Psychotherapy and EMDR, both rooted in
the tradition of mindfulness, may prove useful in helping clients experience a
sense of safety. We know that both a FELT SENSE OF SAFETY and a felt sense of
threat begin prior to perception, at a less than conscious level, so we can remind
clients that all of the autonomic nervous system patterns are in service of survival,
despite how maladaptive or frustrating they are in the moment (Dana, 2018).

But what specific skills will result in reliable improvements over time? A frequently used tool in both medical and psychological treatment, linked to mindfulness, EMDR, and Sensorimotor Psychotherapy, is the technique of deep
breathing, at a slowed pace, while visualizing or being shown one's HRV. In a
study of 112 participants, Laborde et al. (2022) explored the effects of slowed-
pace breathing on HRV and psychological stress indicators. Pre/post assessments
showed decreased emotional valence, lower emotional arousal, increased emotional control, and higher HRV.

In a laboratory experiment with 18 male subjects, Prinsloo et al. (2013) used
lab-induced stress to mirror workplace stress, using two Stroop tasks (a widely
used task of matching colors to words), with subjects randomly split into either
a control group or a biofeedback group that was shown their heart rate during
the second Stroop task. The biofeedback group showed a short-term carryover
effect on HRV, after the rest and lab-induced stress, compared to controls. This
laboratory experiment illustrates what happens in the therapeutic space with
autistic clients: as they become more animated, and the pace of speech and
heart rate increases, they exit mindful awareness and return to their chronic
state of threat.

Güeita-Rodríguez et al. (2021) monitored 64 youth (half with ASD, and half
without) for vagal tone during aquatic therapy and then gave them swimming,
social, emotional, and cognitive tasks. In those with ASD, as vagal tone increased

(e.g., increased HRV), so did social scores in a statistically significant way. In both groups, statistically significant changes occurred in the social, emotional, cognitive, and swimming tasks. This suggests swimming results in deeper, slower breathing, increasing vagal tone, which can modulate both stress and social skills in ASD populations.

The increased sense of safety achieved through slowed breathing, which increases HRV and decreases stress levels, holds implications for how we as therapists work with the autistic mind: How does the therapist engage someone in a chronic state of threat, with actively engaged sympathetic or dorsal vagus nervous systems? In the kindest way possible. To quote Pierre Janet (1925, p. 754) again, "Above all, when we are dealing with [trauma] we must be gentle." While autism is not necessarily trauma induced, it is helpful to think about working with it in a similar way: as gently as possible. A nervous system that is gearing up for survival or actively engaged in threat detection is doing this at a less than conscious level, in a natural process established millennia ago that is less than helpful in the here and now, especially in the therapy space. Thus, a gentle interruption must occur. As Janina Fisher (2017) says in *Healing the Fragmented Selves*, "Processing trauma should not be traumatic." She goes on to articulate that during sessions she will actually interrupt patients during their interchanges, specifically to disrupt their process of trauma. Patients with autism can be thought of in a similar way.

How does one gently interrupt this maladaptive pattern of sympathetic nervous system activation? With my autistic clients, I will sometimes play old (I'm 33) to get them to stop and take a breath. This works especially well with my Gen Z or Gen Alpha patients and will often sound something like, "Could you repeat that a bit slower, my ears can't keep up, they are old." And more often than not my autistic patient will oblige and repeat whatever they just said. I then follow up with the question, "What was that like for you to slow down?" This often induces a mindful interruption much needed by an increasingly activated nervous system. Slowing down to answer the question does two things: it slows the heart rate and slows the breathing. This offers a gentle interruption of a maladaptive pattern: the nervous system entering a threat state through activation of the sympathetic and dorsal vagal systems.

When an autistic client enters therapeutic space, like any other client they bring in some regulating strategies, but much of the work is about interruption of the naturally occurring chronic state of threat. The work of the neural exercise is about flipping the vagal switch through neural exercises related to cultivating safety, to enable clients to come out of their state of threat—allowing their autistic nervous system to come "down the vagal ladder," to borrow a phrase from Deb Dana's work.

BUILDING SOCIAL SKILLS

As discussed throughout this book, generating a sense of safety relates to improving HRV, both in general and in autistic clients. Being able to enter a ventral vagal state of safety also enables improvements in skills directly related to social communication. The effort again is to create a more reliable state of safety by re-flipping the vagal switch.

Higher HRV Improves Nonverbal Social Communication Skills

Anatomically speaking, the vagus or "wandering" nerve is linked to vital social functions. The heart is linked via the cranial nerve to muscles in the middle ears, face (including the eyes), pharynx, larynx, and those that control head movement (see Figure 1.1). The ventral vagal circuit, the newest evolutionary circuit involving pathways within the vagus nerve, is the command center for many of the anatomical features of socialization, controlling such behaviors as facial expression, voice intonation, head turns, detecting the human voice from background sounds, and much more. Thus, increased vagal tone could result in increased social skills.

In 2011 Porges outlined how increased eye contact occurs when humans are in the ventral vagal circuit, explaining how actions like elongated gaze are far more possible when the autonomic nervous system is not in a constant state of threat. As noted throughout, HRV is an indicator of autonomic nervous system state. The autistic autonomic nervous system is substantially less influenced by the ventral vagal system than that of the general population, as has been repeatedly demonstrated (Owens et al., 2021; Parma et al., 2021; Patriquin et al., 2019; Porges, 2005; Porges et al., 2013, 2014). This is consistent with what we might expect in areas effectively controlled by the vagus nerve (as outlined in Figure 8.1), including neck control, eye muscles, and facial controls—all affected differently in those with lower versus higher levels of HRV. In Patriquin et al.'s (2019) comparison sample, tasks involving regions controlled by the vagus nerve (e.g., joint attention affected by neck control) were affected in those with ASD. Thus, a threat response present in those with ASD would affect performance on tasks like social skills and the musculature involved (eyes, head turning, etc.), which are controlled and mediated by the vagus nerve. In short, the body language of these children with ASD communicate that they are in a state of threat.

The lower HRV in this population agrees with their greater risk of not being able to engage in social interdependence. Colizzi et al. (2020) studied COVID-19's longitudinal impacts on children with autism; 78.1% of the over 500 parents surveyed reported difficulties in their children's use of free time, higher risk of more intensive behaviors, and more frequent disruptive behaviors. The year 2020 was a time of increased threat state for just about everyone; this demonstrates how an already stressed nervous system responds under the most stressful of conditions. We should also consider that during this time, as children with ASD experienced even more difficulty, fewer people around them were available to help them co-regulate through and out of this state of threat.

In their work on autism, Patriquin et al. (2019) found higher RSA in toddlers with ASD than in age matched neurotypical controls, suggesting higher HRV is associated with better social skills, joint attention, and language abilities. Thus, we might expect to see the inverse: as HRV decreases (as in Patriquin's sample with ASD), one should expect to see social skills decline, such skills as joint attention, social communication, and language abilities.

Bal et al. (2013) compared RSA and ability to accurately identify basic emotions (e.g., anger, disgust, fear, happiness, sadness, and surprise) between autistic and nonautistic children. Children with autism had lower RSA, identified emotions more slowly, and made more errors in identifying anger. In a similar study, Van Hecke et al. (2009) compared 18 children with autism and 14 nonautistic children 8–12 years of age by monitoring their HRV levels and EEG data while they viewed a video of an unfamiliar person reading them a story. The children with autism had lower RSA levels overall than their nonautistic peers, and "higher RSA was related to higher social skill ratings and fewer problem behaviors" (Van Hecke et. al, 2010). These results support the hypothesis that a cardiac link exists between HRV and social ability: as HRV improves, so too do social skills; as it lowers, social skills deteriorate.

This research implies that if therapists are to help their autistic clients begin to use the vagal brake, the work needs to center on shifting HRV. Previous chapters have suggested a number of modalities that can do this, including mindfulness, slowed breathing, cardiovascular exercise, and motivational interviewing. These mechanisms allow a gentle, repeated shifting from threat to nonthreat states.

Social Work Pedagogy to Improve Social Communication Skills

Social work pedagogy has a crowded field of structured treatments for social skill development, such as the Program for the Enrichment and Education of Relational Skills (PEERS) model (Laugeson et al., 2009; Van Hecke et al., 2015), the Social Communication, Emotional Regulation, and Transactional Support (SCERTS™) model (Prizant et. al, 2006), and the Treatment and Education of Autistic and Related Communication–Handicapped Children (TEAACH) model (Virues-Ortega et al., 2013). The neural exercises described here that relate to social skill development borrow from this tradition, which provides general tools and supporting evidence for their use with both autistic and non-autistic populations.

Role-Playing. One of the signature pedagogical strategies to prepare social work students to work in the field is ROLE-PLAYING: staged interaction involving a prompt, in which one partner plays the client and the other the social work practitioner. Enacted in a classroom situation, role-play becomes an effective tool for modeling appropriate and inappropriate reactions. In a qualitative analysis of social work students through a series of workshops using role-play, students reported feelings of boosted self-esteem (Hitchin, 2016), a key predictor of willingness to take social risks. Robinson (2017) looked at how self-perceptions of acceptability or rejection predicted willingness to take risk; levels of self-esteem correlated with both goal-avoidance and goal-approaching behaviors. Thus, role-play can be a useful practice for building positive self-perception to increase social risk-taking.

How does this practice translate to working with clients on the spectrum? In the field of vocational rehabilitation, adult job seekers with autism are often given mock interviews. Is there actual evidence that this role-play tool is effective in facilitating back-and-forth social interactions? Kumazaki et al. (2019), in a study of nine adults with ASD who took turns being interviewers and interviewees, found improved social skills and self-confidence. This result lends support to the notion that increasing self-esteem translates into improved social skills via improved self-perception in autistic adults. Trudel and Nadig (2019) exposed autistic individuals without intellectual delay and nonautistic individuals to the Role-Play Assessment of Social Skills (R-PASS); as expected, autistic individuals scored substantially lower than controls. Researchers then gave seven autistic individuals a sociodrama intervention to practice social skills, and then they took the R-PASS again, showing statistically significant improvements on social skill abilities. Silva and Silva (2017) filmed six children with autism, four to six years old, in play situations. From their transcribed and coded videos, the researchers found that the adult role in constructing play scenarios was essential to facilitate interaction. Similarly, therapists offer feedback to autistic clients regarding social context, to allow them to develop the nuts and bolts of social interaction, providing the scaffolding necessary to allow self-esteem development and social skill experimentation.

A signature value of social work practice is the *strengths perspective*: focusing on the aspects of a person that enhance their existence, even when those aspects might be seen by others as deficits. Similarly, in our clinical work with clients with ASD, it is important to highlight as strengths the very qualities the world perceives to be weaknesses (e.g., self-soothing behaviors and interests) and to use those strengths to begin the work. For instance, if a client loves trains but struggles in school to write a paper for history, it might be useful to suggest a topic from the world of trains, such as how they connect to the historical development of the Western world. Sometimes, highlighting the very things that family members, teachers, or even friends detest, but the autistic person loves, can in and of itself be an intervention. The work of the therapeutic alliance involves reframing and reimagining the rejections our clients are so often used to encountering, so that we can help them reach their therapeutic goals.

One of the approaches that make social work pedagogy unique is the teacher-student relationship, which tends to be more interactional than typically found in the expert-learner models of other disciplines. Students of social work tend to have a bidirectional relationship with educators, who deliver some expertise but also allow students to offer feedback and questions. This student–educator dyad is similar to the therapeutic alliance: mentorship is part of the dynamic. For clients with autism, we contribute mentorship by modeling social communication skills.

The therapist brings to the therapeutic alliance some expertise in the nuances of communication skills. As part of the great deal of work that goes into getting a clinical license, we sharpen our skills of interacting and inquiry, through clinical classwork, internships, and so on, in order to demonstrate social skills expertise. As we treat our clients with autism, we can deliver that expertise with gentleness and ease.

Integrating social skill development can not only enhance the effectiveness of the therapeutic space but also helps translates these skills for the autistic client to the outer social world. Field instruction in social work pedagogy involves having a social worker who is more experienced work with clients alongside a trainee. In the same way, a therapist, or even a family member or a trusted friend, can play this role to help an autistic individual apply learning to their actual social world and can then provide a safe space for reflection.

It can be useful to coordinate with a loved one (mother, brother, etc.) to provide a social space outside of the therapy room to help your client generalize these newly found social skills. This provides an additional lens or vantage point through which to provide feedback to the autistic client on their social skill development. While ideally this role of social mentoring is occupied by a loved one, this is not always feasible in clinical practice and thus may require additional work on the part of the therapist. It is critical to continually assess whether the client is asking for feedback or not.

It may feel strange to bring oneself into the room, so to speak—to attempt to enter the space with no hidden intentions, but a clear intention to help with an ounce of who we are outside the therapeutic space that can be felt in a deep and genuine way. But it is a core part of helping with people who struggle socially to be able to reflect and critically think with feedback on what might work better socially.

Motivational Interviewing. Another pedagogical strategy in social work and clinical psychology pedagogy is the skill of MOTIVATIONAL INTERVIEWING, the only strategy offered here that is concerned with change talk in the client. It is not within the scope of this text to completely cover motivational interviewing— much like other modalities, it is a skill therapists can develop to varying levels, from basic through advanced. This brief description introduces a much deeper practice that is widely accepted as an evidence-based strategy in a number of fields, including health care, recovery, vocational rehabilitation, and customer service. I also include some recommendations for further reading at the end of this chapter. Training in motivational interviewing is widely available, and clinicians should have at least a basic skill level before employing it in practice.

As defined by its creators, "Motivational Interviewing is a particular way of having a conversation about change so that it is the client rather than the clinician who *voices the arguments for change*" (Arkowitz et al., 2008). It is most commonly operationalized across a process of open-ended questions, affirmations, reflections, and summaries, a skill base known as OARS:

> *Open-ended questions*: Posing questions in such a way that clients have wide latitude in how to respond
> *Affirmations:* Recognizing positive steps and achievements
> *Reflections:* Communicating accurate empathy, comprising either repetitions of a client's statements or guesses at what a client feels but has not yet expressed
> *Summaries:* Synthesizing themes and putting emphasis on certain points or statements the client has made

The practice of this set of skills emphasizes client choice and autonomy in conducting conversations about change.

Using this skill set has repeatedly been shown to improve the therapeutic alliance with clients with autism. In *The Great Psychotherapy Debate* (Wampold & Imel, 2015), Bruce Wampold offers a meta-analysis of factors that affect outcome in therapies, with effect sizes of for factors: goal consensus (0.7), empathy (0.6), alliance (0.6), positive regard (0.6), congruence (0.5), treatment differences (0.2), competence (0.2), adherence to protocol (0.1), and specific ingredients (0.05). This demonstrates the power of the therapeutic alliance in working with the client: not modality or specific technique but factors like goal consensus and alliance lead to positive outcomes positive with effect sizes of 0.6 and 0.7—difference in therapeutic approach has only a 0.2 effect size.

IMPLICATIONS

The end goals of each of these neural exercises tools are to engage in meaningful social development of autistic individuals and to allow these clients greater access to a felt sense of safety. Cultivation of safety and building of social communication skills through this Polyvagal Theory–informed, gentle approach can begin to improve VAGAL EFFICIENCY, strengthening the vagal switch in the CARDIO-INHIBITORY PATHWAY. Being gentle and reflective, with the right amount of scaffolding, gives a person in a chronic state of threat the opportunity to venture outside of this constant state of fear and, as they become less afraid, to develop the skills to build self-esteem and strengthen self-confidence.

FURTHER READING ON MOTIVATIONAL INTERVIEWING AND AUTISM

Alter, C. (2012, July 1). Motivational interviewing: A useful approach for families and counselors for post-secondary transitions. *Autism Spectrum News.* https://autismspectrumnews.org/motivational-interviewing-a-useful-approach-for-families-and-counselors-planning-for-post-secondary-transition/

Bellesheim, K. R., Cole, L., Coury, D. L., Yin, L., Levy, S. E., Guinnee, M. A., Klatka, K., Malow, B. A., Katz, T., Taylor, J., & Sohl, K. (2018). Family-driven goals to improve care for children with autism spectrum disorder. *Pediatrics, 142*(3), e20173225.

de Jong, R. K., Snoek, H., Staal, W. G., & Klip, H. (2019). The effect of patients' feedback on treatment outcome in a child and adolescent psychiatric sample: A randomized controlled trial. *European Child and Adolescent Psychiatry, 28*(6), 819–834. https://doi.org/10.1007/s00787-018-1247-4

Hartman, E., Schlegelmilch, A., Roskowski, M., Anderson, C. A., & Tansey, T. N. (2019). Early findings from the Wisconsin PROMISE Project: Implications for policy and practice. *Journal of Vocational Rehabilitation, 51*(2), 167–181.

Keeley, R. D., Burke, B. L., Brody, D., Dimidjian, S., Engel, M., Emsermann, C., deGruy, F., Thomas, M., Moralez, E., Koester, S., & Kaplan, J. (2014). Training to use motivational interviewing techniques for depression: A cluster randomized trial. *Journal of the American Board of Family Medicine, 27*(5), 621–36. https://doi.org/10.3122/jabfm.2014.05.130324

New Focus Academy. (2020, September 21). What is motivational interviewing and how does it help teens on the spectrum? https://newfocusacademy.com/what-is-motivational-interviewing-and-how-does-it-help-teens-on-the-spectrum/

Wampold, B. E., & Imel, Z. E. (2015). *The great psychotherapy debate: The evidence for what makes psychotherapy work* (2nd ed.). Routledge/Taylor and Francis Group.

Wetherby, A. M. (2017–2022). Autism adaptive community-based treatment to improve outcomes using Navigators (ACTION) Network
(NIH grant). https://grantome.com/grant/NIH/R01-HD093055-03

CHAPTER 9

Exercises for Finding Safety

....

*Thus, to fulfill our biological imperative of connectedness,
our personal agenda needs to be directed toward making
individuals feel safe.*

> STEPHEN W. PORGES, *THE POCKET GUIDE TO THE
> POLYVAGAL THEORY*

As discussed throughout the previous chapters, human beings have a FELT SENSE OF SAFETY when they enter the ventral vagal state. A repeatedly demonstrated concept in the research literature is that deep breathing, often with biofeedback, can yield change in vagal states. Here the primary application of that concept involves teaching clients to practice slower exhalations relative to short inhalations. While the concept is not overtly complex, the practice often involves entering a part of the nervous system that is foreign to the autistic self. This chapter explores how to integrate into therapy meaningful ways to cultivate a sense of safety by strengthening the vagal brake.

Part of what makes living with autism so challenging for so many of my clients is how fast their mind operates—a reflection of a chronically engaged state of threat. In short, communication difficulties are actually the by-product of living in the dorsal and sympathetic states. Take the client who tried to teach me how to solve a Rubik's Cube. When we started, he would say things like, "Turn the three white parts of the cube left and toward you," and I would just look at him blankly. Questions running through my mind were, *Does he mean his left, or my left? Which three parts is he talking about?*

This example highlights a characteristic expectation in the mind of an autistic individual: that other people should understand what they are talking about, without explanation. Autistic brains move fast and communicate poorly. Some of my autistic peers will say that communication breakdown occurs only between autistic and nonautistic minds, implying that neurotypical individuals need to keep up, but autistic people at most make up 2% of some countries' population (e.g., the United States), so that expectation is unrealistic—and contrary to most of our clients' goals to develop stronger social skills. Some may say this is an ableist position, but an important adaptation for people with autism who wish to coexist with the general population is being able to come out of a threat state long enough to slow down, to feel safe enough to risk communication, and to develop an understanding of when comfortable communication, or a feeling of safety, is breaking down.

BREATHE SLOWLY

"Breathe slow, someone help me breathe slow"—Chelsea Cutler sings this in her 2018 song "Hell." There is tremendous power in breathing slowly in the face of psychological pain. She longs for a reprieve from the pain of missing her lover and from the agony of pain receptors in her brain giving her a physical experience of social rejection. In the same way, the breath can unlock the mysterious vagal brake that allows the autistic nervous system to enter a state of safety.

APPLYING A SENSE OF SAFETY TO INCREASE SOCIAL COMMUNICATION SKILLS

From a clinical standpoint it is useful to think about how information is organized in the nervous system of an autistic person. Chapter 2 introduced the core organizers for information processing often referred to as the "Five MICE" (see Table 2.1): the five senses, movement, inner sensations, cognitions, and emotions (Ogden et al., 2006). Within the context of Sensorimotor Psychotherapy, these organizers can help clients understand their experience of their body by drawing on one of these five points of reference. Different therapeutic approaches sequence these organizers differently.

In the therapeutic space, however, you will likely notice your autistic clients tend to move from cognition down to emotion, if we are lucky, and more often just stay cognitive. To cultivate safety, it is important how we link the experience of autistic clients to this new experience. Thus, by starting with a bodily approach, the therapist performs an essential balancing act, pushing back on the purely rational reflex of the autistic mind in order to engage with sensations of the body, the movements it may make, the emotions it may express, and the potentially hyper- or hypoaroused five senses. An act of therapy to experience safety thus comes from connecting the autistic mind to these less familiar, and at times uncomfortable, but necessary states where safety is experienced.

From an EMDR perspective, in contrast, information processing is conceptualized as happening in the reverse order: first cognitively, then emotionally, and then finally in the body, which in some ways mirrors the information processing of our autistic clients. The discussion in the rest of this chapter assumes this order, working cognitively, then emotionally, and then somatically with clients. In my own clinical experience, clients with autism tend to rely on cognition as the most adaptive of strategies, often at the expense of other systems, like emotional and somatic knowing, so this can be a good entry point to build a therapeutic alliance.

For more cognitively capable clients, such as many autistic adults, mindfulness can be applied in a cognitive fashion first and then extrapolated on and deepened with emotional and somatic strategies. To borrow a metaphor from the work of Deb Dana (2020) in translating Polyvagal Theory, the autistic nervous system goes up and down the "vagal ladder." As discussed in previous chapters, our beliefs about self, others, and the world often shift based on the state of our autonomic nervous system. A client who is socially engaged, for instance, might express such beliefs as "I'm okay," "people are okay," and "the world is an okay place." If that same client is in a state of fight/flight, those beliefs instead might be "I'm pissed," "people are idiots," and "the world is going to pieces." In collapse, those beliefs might change to "I'm defeated," "people are mean," and "the world is a cruel place." We can encourage our autistic clients toward being able to notice how these beliefs sound and feel in the different states of social engagement, fight/flight, and collapse. By listing these out, autistic clients can begin to apply this new awareness of their own state at various points throughout the day, for example, the beliefs present while teaching a class, versus beliefs present while driving in heavy traffic. This new level of awareness, of noticing where on the vagal ladder one actually is at specific moments, gives our clients a better sense of which states they occupy most of the time.

This COGNITIVE SCAFFOLDING, or *the necessary cognitive support needed to assist a client move from what they can do to what they want to do*, involving providing a cognitive way to experience emotions first, can be helpful to steeping a person into the experience. Introducing this cognitive scaffolding in a mindful way, much like a clinician working within an internal family systems lens, helps autistic clients begin to conceptualize how safety might be experienced emotionally and somatically. As autistic clients introduce narratives to the clinician and identify varied nervous system states, it can be simple to introduce cognitive appraisal of the different states using the many and varied forms of emotional vocabulary. Paul Ekman's *Atlas of Emotion*, one of the more popular references, free and accessible online, offers an emotional vocabulary for sessions. For younger clients you can pull emotion vocabulary and even colors from the popular Zones of Regulation Tool (Kuypers, 2011). Regardless of how these emotions are labeled, cognitive appraisal of emotions encourages children and adults on the spectrum to interact with this emotional way of knowing. This allows them to begin noticing their nervous system with more nuanced progressions of safety, fight/flight, and freeze, expanding into a vagal ladder colored with sadness, anger, happiness, joy, or even peace.

SOMATIC AWARENESS

Just as the cognitive and emotional ways of knowing can be strengthened, so can deeper somatic ways of knowing. I cannot stress enough how helpful the trainings of Dr. Pat Ogden and Dr. Peter Levine can be in integrating somatic awareness into therapeutic practice. My hope is that this brief introduction into somatic psychology encourages you to explore its depths further.

Clients on the spectrum often meet the somatic way of knowing with a fair amount of resistance—the result of having to adapt to dealing with the shame of being different. Often these clients place a fair amount of reliance on cognition, often at the expense of bodily awareness. Thus, the autistic individual often experiences repeated alienation from sensorimotor experience. Because of this, somatic awareness may actually be the most difficult to cultivate, using core organizers like movements or five-sense perception or another body-centered approach (Ogden et al., 2006; Ogden & Fisher, 2015; Ogden et al., 2021). Somatic psychotherapy approaches recommended here should not be considered a comprehensive way to address deficits in interoception as research on the effectiveness of this type of psychology is limited in ASD patients.

That said, somatic awareness has rather practical treatment strategies. As the research literature indicates, it is relatively easy to increase heart rate variability (HRV) to a statistically significant level, through biofeedback monitoring and deep breathing. The therapist working to build social communication skills can be thought of as helping clients breathe slowly in order to activate the vagal brake. From the perspective of this book, the therapist is the expert on slow breathing, and the client is the expert on how the breathing is affecting them.

When introducing deep breathing in my own clinical practice, I often have autistic clients place their hands on their heart. This feels like being given a hug, neurologically speaking. A hand on their chest as they take a breath gives them a way to connect with several of the five core organizers (Ogden et al., 2006; Ogden & Fisher, 2015; Ogden et al., 2021) and to engage in grounding through the use of their body. Ideally this changes a problematic, historical relationship with a body in a frequent state of threat and lack of safety. This offers a pathway for clinical work to begin building connections between experiences of safety and the autistic physical body. The introduction of deep breathing can be paired with previously introduced concepts like cognitive scaffolding and emotional appraisal, skills that rely on older adaptive strategies.

For somatosensory appraisal, Figure 9.1 lists vocabulary terms (Ogden & Fisher, 2015) for sensations that can help clients with autism, who often have limited vocabularies related not only to emotional experience but also to somatic experience. This can be used to provide scaffolding to clients who struggle to identify what words are linked to their internal physical experience. Interoception is a well noted challenge in the autistic population, so this tool can be a useful addition as you work with clients to connect to their bodies, when they have limited experiences doing so in a positive way, so that they can become more aware of their nervous system states.

VOCABULARY FOR SENSATIONS

achy	clenched	energized	itchy	puffy	tense
airy	congested	faint	jerky	quaking	thick
bloated	constricted	flaccid	jumbly	quivery	tickly

blocked	cool	floaty	knotted	radiating	tight
breathless	cold	fluid	light	sharp	tingly
bubbly	damp	flushed	moist	shivery	trembling
burning	dense	fluttery	nauseous	shuddering	twitchy
buzzy	dizzy	fuzzy	numb	sore	vibrating
chills	dull	goose-bumps	paralyzed	stiff	warm
churning	electric	heavy	pins and needles	suffocating	weak
clammy	empty	hot	prickly	sweaty	wobbly

Source: From SENSORIMOTOR PSYCHOTHERAPY: INTERVENTIONS FOR TRAUMA AND ATTACHMENT by Pat Ogden and Janina Fisher. Copyright © by Pat Ogden. Used by permission of W. W. Norton & Company, Inc. Adapted from Ogden, P. (1997, 1998).

EXECUTIVE FUNCTIONING INTERVENTIONS

While thus far we have focused on ways to help clients cope during sessions, to enable them to practice skills in a safe therapeutic space, we now shift our attention to how safety can help children with ASD who struggle with EF skills. As clients with ASD repeatedly experience moments of a felt sense of safety and improve their ability to come down the vagal ladder, they have greater access to planning skills necessary to organize and coordinate our world, which can present an unfamiliar challenge. Developmental theorists have long discussed how to address this challenge. For instance, many in our field are familiar with developmental psychologist Lev Vygotsky's description of the space between what a learner can do and what a learner needs help to do: the *zone of proximal development* (Berk & Winsler, 1995). Another important concept is Barkley's theory of executive functioning, introduced in Chapter 2. This section again explores this theory, in the context of generating and maintaining a felt sense of safety.

To reiterate, EXECUTIVE FUNCTIONING (EF) as defined by Barkley (2010, 2012) is "self-regulation across time for the attainment of one's goals (self-interests), often in the context of others." EF is a metaconstruct that encompasses the constructs of self-management/time, self-organization/problem solving, self-restraint, self-motivation, and self-regulation of emotions. These five areas are the building blocks to organize our experiences, at home, at school, at work, and in public. The case example below explores how a therapist provides consultation for a parent about selecting an intervention, by using the five constructs within the EF metaconstruct to help the parent formulate guiding questions and hypotheses, to collect more data from the teacher about the child's needs.

GUIDING QUESTIONS about how children on the autism spectrum function, in school and home tasks, help us collect information about what EF challenges a kid on the spectrum faces. HYPOTHESES typically are educated guesses we make so that we can test whether our ideas are true or false (in science) or more accurate or less accurate, in the context of a Polyvagal Theory of ASD. Guiding questions then help test the hypotheses, to identify challenges that are barriers to kids moving down the vagal ladder and to suggest strategies to help them achieve that goal. (See Figure 8.1.)

Building on the understanding of a polyvagal model of ASD you did with the child on the spectrum, family member, or caregiver, let's begin to formulate some guiding questions and hypotheses to test how to bring this autistic child down the vagal ladder.

Case Example: Billy

A parent of Billy, a 9-year-old autistic boy and a client of mine, received an email from his fourth-grade teacher:

> Dear . . .
>
> I just wanted to reach out to let you know I'm having some issues with Billy's attention.
>
> He's bringing some small toys into the room and playing during instruction. When the toys are removed, he finds other things to play with. Then when it comes to work time, he gets frustrated because he doesn't know what to do.
>
> I was just hoping you and/or mom can have a chat with him about what you expect of him, so we're on the same page.
>
> If you have any questions, please let me know.
>
> Thank you . . .

Presenting Problem

In this case 9-year-old Billy remains in a constant state of threat, owing to his ASD, and struggles to attend to what is actually happening in the present moment, likely from both a lack of bodily awareness and a need to daydream. This lack of attending, while a minor issue in years before, is compounded by the fact that Billy needs to grasp these EF skills for his transition to middle school in fifth grade. Thus, it is relevant to his psychological well-being to learn to self-regulate in a more present way, not least to avoid the frustration of failure when he cannot complete the assignments.

Intervention

Billy's parent, concerned, comes in to ask what we do for Billy: How do we help him pay attention? First I helped him break down the problem of inattention in terms of its root causes. We *hypothesized* that inattention might include one or two potential causes for these dysregulated responses: *boredom* or *too much energy*. Combining a Polyvagal Theory lens and Barkley's EF constructs (self-management/time, self-organization/problem solving, self-restraint, self-motivation, and self-regulation/emotions), we considered that boredom might involve challenges with emotional self-regulation and self-motivation, and too much energy might involve challenges with emotional self-regulation and self-restraint.

To test these hypotheses, we decided to pose the following *guiding questions* for the teacher to ask herself when she sees Billy playing rather than learning, that is, having an inattentive episode:

1. Is Billy struggling to focus in class because he is bored (lack of emotional regulation, lack of motivation)?
2. Is Billy struggling to focus in class because he has an overabundance of energy (lack of emotional regulation, lack of self-restraint)?

Test Hypothesis 1: Boredom—Strategies to Increase Attention

> *Strategy 1*: Increasing Billy's motivation through direct consequences
> *Strategy 2*: Increasing Billy's emotional regulation through movement
> *Strategy 3*: Increasing Billy's emotional regulation through fidgets

Test Hypothesis 2: Overabundance of Energy—Strategies to Increase Attention

> *Strategy 4*: Increasing Billy's emotional regulation through movement

Strategy 5: Increasing Billy's self-restraint through potential for
direct consequences

The final step was then for me to share these guiding questions and
strategies with the teacher to use when Billy is having an inattentive
episode. Depending on her answers to the questions, she can try different strategies during classroom learning, taking data on incidents of
distractibility.

Based on feedback from the teacher, she ended up relying heavily
on standing desks (Strategies 2 and 4) and allowing Billy to use erasers
to engage in limited imaginary play when he was bored (a version of
Strategy 3)—this improved his productivity, in the teacher's eyes, by
50–75%, and she considered it a success.

IMPLICATIONS

While perhaps not as emotionally oriented or cognitively oriented, this example
represents the need for ways to cultivate safety for ASD nervous systems that
allow them to achieve important developmental milestones, like attending due
to increased joint attention through simple play interventions.

The EF intervention described above is manualized as a neural exercise at the
end of this chapter, for use directly with clients. This worksheet breaks down
how to apply this EF intervention in a guided way, rooted in a polyvagal model
of ASD, to explore how to address social challenges encountered by those with
ASD.

Neural Exercise: Cultivating Safety Through Executive Functioning

EXECUTIVE FUNCTIONING (EF) is defined by Barkley (2010, 2012) as "self-regulation across time for the attainment of one's goals (self-interests), often in the context of others." The EF META-CONSTRUCT covers the skills of self-management of time, self-organization/problem solving, self-restraint, self-motivation, and self-regulation of emotions.

What is the educational or parental concern raised regarding the child's behavior? _____

_____

_____

_____

_____

_____

_____

_____

_____

What hypotheses might account for this child's inability to regulate this developmental task? Which of Barkley's EF challenges might affect this child's ability to regulate this developmental task?
Hypothesis 1: _____

_____

☐ self-management/time, ☐ self-organization/problem solving,
☐ self-restraint, ☐ self-motivation, ☐ emotional self-regulation
Hypothesis 2: _____

_____

☐ self-management/time, ☐ self-organization/problem solving,
☐ self-restraint, ☐ self-motivation, ☐ emotional self-regulation

What guiding questions can we ask to shape our strategies to help this child face this social task?

Question 1: _____

_____

_____

_____

_____

_____

Question 2: _____

_____

_____

_____

_____

_____

Strategies/interventions for Question 1:

Strategy 1: _____

_____

_____

Strategy 2: _____

_____

_____

Strategies/interventions for Question 2:

Strategy 3: _____

_____

_____

Strategy 4: _____

_____

_____

When you tried this, what did you learn?
Question 1: _____
    Strategy 1: _____
    Strategy 2: _____
Question 2: _____
    Strategy 3: _____
    Strategy 4: _____

Repeat this worksheet to narrow down the hypotheses and fine-tune your strategies. Continue until you have found workable solutions. Repeat in the future if new strategies are needed.

CHAPTER 10

Exercises to Build Social Communication Skills

Your emotions grow out of your relational history. Even if you've had the most adverse set of early experiences, when you immerse yourself in new relationships with space for mismatch and repair, meanings of hopelessness can be transformed into meanings of hope.

ED TRONICK, *THE POWER OF DISCORD*

Tronick's words stick with me because he makes space for failure in relationships and ways to come back from it. In his research he highlights that relationships experience failure, repair, and reconnection. It is within this space of ups and downs, rights and lefts—for autistic people, therapists, parents, and educators—that hope can be found.

Hope is often a difficult thing to find as a person with autism. In one session a client on the spectrum wasn't present in the waiting room as expected—he emerged from the bathroom in tears. It's still unclear to me to this day why he was crying, but after inviting him back into my office he sat down, pushed his face into the couch, and cried.

He did this for the better part of thirty minutes. He then pro-
ceeded to tell me it wasn't a big deal, and he was being overly sensitive.
I replied, "Why do you keep gaslighting yourself?" Again his response
was defensive—his nervous system wasn't ready to hear what I shared.
It was in a defensive state, and I missed that because of the counter-
transference occurring through the helping impulse.

There are times where repair is not the way to go. Moving away from rupture is
a natural human impulse, but in this scenario trying to intervene was more about
me than him. It was about trying to ease the suffering of another human nervous
system. But as Sensorimotor Psychotherapy Institute trainer Patrick Weeg said,
"Don't rescue them from the silence." This statement is hauntingly true. Healing
and hope come from within—as therapists, parents, and teachers, we are noth-
ing more than the context within which this hope can occur, to paraphrase Ron
Kurtz's quote from Chapter 2. Thus, it becomes the task of therapy with a person
on the spectrum to form a dynamic relationship in which they can be critical of
us and we can provide feedback to them from an open and honest place. It is in
this place, where the rupture can be tolerated—because of the expectation of
repair and attunement—that we should begin to create a more reliable state of
safety so they have the space to unpack the challenges they face.

APPLYING SOCIAL WORK AND PSYCHOLOGICAL PEDAGOGY

Social work has a rich tradition of focusing on clients' strengths. Granted, some
social workers are more cynical than others, but as a profession the emphasis is on
the positive attributes and skills of human beings. Similarly, this book embraces
the perspective that people on the spectrum not only have inherent worth and
value but also possess valuable skills, talents, and interests that can be effective
entry points for both the therapeutic alliance and therapeutic approaches. This is
a far more effective way to protect the hard-won disability rights of those with
ASD than to adopt a social model of disability like neurodiversity that doesn't
recognize the need for treatment. It would be naive to think that employers and
schools will continue to honor the needs of individuals with autism if we don't
root those needs in an evidence-based framework. The beauty of the Polyvagal
Theory of ASD and the visceromotor approach to therapy is that they posit no

"cause" or "cure" but, rather, offer known approaches to alleviate challenges that anyone with low HRV may face, regardless of etiology.

It is both possible and necessary to adopt a strengths perspective on human worth, as social work has so richly done for over a century, and marry it with research showing that the autonomic nervous system of autistic individuals is in a chronic state of threat. By moving in this direction, we not only protect our accommodations but also do not suggest that, in the relationship between the autistic individual and the rest of the world, the world is the only one in the relationship that needs to change. A polyvagal approach to autism abandons the social model of disability in favor of a social work and psychology pedagogy that introduces dignity and worth to the autonomic nervous system, to begin to alleviate a chronic state of threat.

Cultivating Verbal and Nonverbal Social Communication

As discussed throughout this book, activation of the social engagement system largely requires a state of safety. This section focuses on building self-esteem as a reliable modality for cultivating social communication. People with autism internalize a lack of acceptance of themselves from a very early age and use masking as an adaptive strategy, hiding and suppressing their natural responses in order to fit in.

This pattern usually emerges after an experience of rejection significant enough to create the need for masking in order to survive and avoid the adverse experience. Over the long haul, masking is internalized, and the effect is far more about the autistic person not accepting themselves than about fear of actually showing the true self. This is what internal family systems therapy would call an *exile*: the part other parts show up to protect, managing the pain so it doesn't reach the exile. In either Sensorimotor Psychotherapy or internal family systems therapy, masking might be considered a form of internalized self-alienation. This internalized shame often shows up in the body of an autistic individual—the alienation from one's own feelings can be experienced through physically harmful effects.

Social work pedagogy provides a narrative form of therapy in which therapists work to normalize and validate the client's experience in terms of both thoughts and feelings. The strategy is to help them befriend their own nervous system, thus teaching clients a new way of being. The sheer act of applying unconditional positive regard as a tool for entrance into the therapeutic alliance is one of the single most important ways social work is embodied. Another tool for building the alliance is viewing the client through a strengths perspective, an approach that does not discount the weaknesses in the autistic person but, rather, intentionally highlights what our autistic clients are good at, in a genuine way.

As the client's window of tolerance (Ogden et al., 2000) for their own social failures opens further, the therapist can offer constructive feedback—think of it as a form of shaping. Again, the therapist is the expert on social skills in the relationship, and the autistic client is the one who decides what type of social skills to attempt. The work of socialization then becomes a collaborative effort between therapist and client to experiment with new social strategies in session, which can then be tested outside the therapy space. Through the trial and error of experimentation, as you both apply these strategies in the therapeutic space, clients develop new social skills they can use throughout their life.

Measuring Increases in Verbal and Nonverbal Social Communication

It remains unclear whether alexithymia, or the inability to access one's own feelings, is a modifiable trait, but with an increased FELT SENSE OF SAFETY, increased emotional awareness can theoretically occur, as the vagal brake is repeatedly engaged. As outlined in Chapter 2, several tools are available to clinically evaluate change related to emotional awareness, on both an energetic and sensation level. With respect to exploring the more energetic awareness of ASD patients, I recommend the TAS-20 (TORONTO ALEXITHYMIA SCALE 20), which includes the General Alexithymia Factor Score Calculator (GAFS-8), an 8-score composite measure of alexithymia. The TAS-20 has demonstrated some validity in ASD populations, but in my opinion it is far more useful for understanding how autism intersects with awareness features involved identifying processes, describing processes, and extrinsically oriented thinking. The GAFS-8 provides a more accurate overall level of alexithymia, even though it has no subscales and does not help explain the difficulty in functioning to an autistic person. Thus, using both the TAS-20 and the GAFS-8 will help both you and your clients make sense of their energetic awareness of emotions through the construct of alexithymia.

With respect to the more somatic awareness of bodily perceptions and their connectivity of emotional experience, Chapter 2 introduced the Body Perception Questionnaire (BPQ) created by Dr. Porges and his team for their work in Polyvagal Theory, which helps the therapeutic dyad understand somatic awareness (or lack thereof) in autistic clients but also provides a helpful screener for more medically based concerns like chest and stomach pains.

AUTISM AND UNMASKING

MASKING, the act of camouflaging the self to fit in socially, is more likely to be practiced in people with autism who require less support, have more awareness of social stigma, are female, have experienced bullying, and have a specific goal in mind, like obtaining a job (Drake, 2022). For autistic individuals this camouflaging often includes trying to hide symptoms associated with ASD, such as stimming behaviors, linguistic challenges, and sensory sensitivities. Masking essentially means muting the self—how does this affect the need for safety?

It is not a question of whether masking is good or bad, and from a polyvagal lens such an either/or approach misses the point entirely. For some proponents of a more social model of disability, masking is seen as an inherently negative approach. As autistic self-advocate and board-certified autism specialist Lisa Morgan (Inderbitzen & Morgan, 2023) argues in her article "Different Brains,"

> While camouflaging can help someone blend in and succeed at work, like it helps animals to stay hidden and not be eaten, the goal for many autistic people is broader than just merely survival. Many autistic people want to belong and to be a part of the workplace where they spend so much of their time. As well, being part of a workplace, making connections, can help their overall success.

To many this view of masking as part of muting a person's identity is accompanied by the belief that autistic people have the right to express their true selves without negative consequences—that ultimately society must accept autistic individuals "as they are." This belief cannot reliably be applied to any individual or group—we all learn and adapt, whether effective or not, throughout our lifetime—and will not benefit most of our clients in their daily lives. In addition it is highly dependent on one's country of origin; take for instance the United States, where the ADA and IDEA law require proof of disability, whereas countries like Canada do not in order to get support and acceptance of needs. These needs are not free of economics and governments and have to be thought of in context. If anything, the expectation that the world, not us, needs to change is a great recipe for failure.

Masking increases suicidal ideation in persons with autism (Cassidy et al., 2020; Inderbitzen & Morgan 2023). And her story is quite moving. As a survivor of suicide attempts, with several family members who succeeded in dying by suicide, she has made a career in both research and practice of working with folks on the autism spectrum in crisis intervention work (Morgan, 2023). Her stance that masking is less than helpful in the context of suicidal ideations (Morgan, 2023) is probably accurate. But this is only one part of the clinical story.

The ability to mask, to blend in or mirror, is a skill central to most forms of social interaction—job interviews, romantic entanglement, any socially nuanced situation that may require temporarily holding back parts of oneself at appropriate moments during the interaction. In the context of treatment, however, clinicians can kindly and gently hold a safe space for clients to express every part of themselves and to explore the parts that they usually hold back. Being effective at using this set of social skills means accurately perceiving others' social cues and our own mental, physical, and emotional reactions to them, usually while jointly cognitively processing words; gauging how we feel in response if one can tolerate feelings; and judging how, and how much, to express, to varying extents as the moment's circumstances change. Anyone who can do this well would not be considered to be masking at all, merely communicating well. Clients with ASD face challenges with each of these elements and can struggle with social communication—getting stuck with masks they can't alter or remove, yet are not effective for them.

Autistic clients often come to treatment in search of a more effective emotional and social filter for the world. Thus, a mix of openness to explore their needs for filters, and encouragement of responsive, temporary muting can help clients operate within the social worlds they occupy. There can be no simple or one-size-fits-all strategies, which instead must be tailored to each client's specific goals and needs.

Of the seven values in this Polyvagal Theory–informed approach to treating autistic clients, the quality of KINDNESS can mediate this clinical decision. This helps us acknowledge that the parts of the autistic self responsible for masking are self-protective in nature, seeking with good intent to shield the autistic person despite how misguided those efforts may be. As Richard

Schwartz (2021) says succinctly, there are "no bad parts." A polyvagal lens does not reflect the masking parts as good or bad but, rather, adaptive or maladaptive, either lending their internal wisdom to help clients adapt to the social context of their lives, or misguiding clients with an overdose of muting, overwhelm, and meltdowns.

Case Example: Emma

One Tuesday morning, Emma arrived at the office, well-groomed and well dressed. An autistic, Christian woman who has been a stay-at-home mother of two boys for nearly a decade, Emma came in reporting her husband had decided to leave. As we dug into her story, she shared, "I'd like to heal." Puzzled, I looked at her softly and asked, "What do you mean by that?" "I don't know exactly," she replied.

It turned out her husband had bipolar disorder and consistently had periods of not taking his medication. During these times, he would make rash purchases and threaten to kill himself because he would be better off dead. Frustrated with him, she had begun the filing for divorce but was not entirely able to move through the process.

In the next session she reported that her husband had started a new job and had started going back and forth between their marital home and his mother's home. As he transitioned back and forth, Emma became increasingly concerned. As she shared in our session rather abruptly, "And then, he went to his mom's, got a new job, and now he wants us to come live with him there." Not entirely understanding why she appeared this agitated, I calmly responded, "Could you repeat that? My ears didn't catch that."

She responded, just a little more slowly, "And then, he went to his mom's, where he got a new job at Burger King, and left his old job. He wants us to come live with him at his mom's, and I'm not entirely sure I want to do that."

I looked at her and asked, "What are you so nervous about?" "Why do you think I'm nervous?" "Well, for one thing," I answered, "your word speed is like 90 words per minute, and how fast we talk tends to reflect what is going on inside us." She looked at me, eyes narrowed, cheeks blushing a soft shade of red, and paused. "I am." "You are?" "I am nervous. And I don't really understand why." With that a timer went off and rather abruptly brought our session to a close. I replied, "Well maybe we can talk about this next time?" "Sure," she replied.

Next week at the start of session, Emma was rather reserved. I could sense something was off, and so I asked, "What's not working for you today?" She looked at me and her shoulders and neck began to turn red. After remaining quiet for a minute, I asked, "Do you feel like you have enough time in session?" "No." She replied rather quickly, "I always feel like I'm in such a rush to tell you everything, and I want to make sure I don't run out of time." Pausing for a moment, I replied, "Well then why can't you tell me that?" "I don't know," she said, looking downward. "Well, if you are going to make it through this divorce, I think therapy should better suit your needs. What if we increased the length of sessions to 90 minutes from now on?"

Presenting Problem

While the problem Emma shared with me was that she wanted to go through with the divorce, this was actually not the only problem she brought into the room. The bigger problem was that she was in a constant state of flight, and this played out in a number of ways she transferred to me: the pace of her story, the inability to voice how frustrated she was, and her lack of response. Emma faced not just a divorce but a relational pattern of experience where she was not allowed to speak up in favor of her own needs. She felt an unconscious push to state those needs as quickly as possible, as if someone were looming over her to punish her.

Intervention

The intervention in this case was twofold: acknowledging the energy Emma brought to the room and naming the power dynamic and how I as her therapist might not be supporting her. While it feels counterintuitive to stop someone who is speaking in therapy, as I was listening to Emma's speed of speech I was picking up on some of the unspoken dynamics present in the room. A person's pace or speed of thought tells us a great deal about the state of their internal world. By my observing her and then asking her to repeat herself, Emma did two things: become more aware and provide more information. She became more mindful as she actually had to think and reflect on what she was saying to me. A mindful state, as discussed throughout this book, is a good way to get clients to enter a less collapsed state and slowly try to turn on the light switch of connection. Repeating herself also forced Emma to provide more information and slow her speech down in an effort to be mindful of how slowly my own brain moved in this scenario, and in so doing found more space to provide information.

The second half of this intervention and reframing is acknowledging the power dynamic. Emma, with a repeated experience of not having her words validated, needed me to actually name the experience of our sessions being too short for her to feel safe enough to let her guard down. That vagal brake needed prompting not in an obtuse way but, rather, with a gentle, open-ended question that allowed her to name her visibly displayed frustration, which in other scenarios might have caused trouble with others. It's a seemingly simple thing to ask what is wrong, and to try to make an educated guess when an open-ended question does not work at first. With Emma, this gave her both the space to answer the question and enough felt sense of safety to do so. And while this experience may seem small, it has made a huge difference in the relational dynamic: Emma can now disclose to me when she is uncomfortable or disagrees with something I say. That she can do so is a measure of her felt sense of safety, which runs so very contrary to her experience with her husband and the relational space she has occupied for nearly a decade.

IMPLICATIONS

Building a vagal brake to move from a threat state to a nonthreat state takes time and effort. It also requires gentleness with autistic clients as we try to understand the often unspoken elements within the room. In many ways the therapeutic alliance itself is the intervention: It creates a space in which clients can repeatedly experience safety, and this safe space allows our autistic clients to begin to let down their guard. To an autistic person with a chronically overactive nervous system, experiencing gentle treatment can feel quite foreign—by simply introducing kindness and gentleness, repeatedly, reliably, we begin to disrupt this chronic state of threat.

Just the Beginning

···

A poet is an unhappy being whose heart is torn by secret
sufferings, but whose lips are so strangely formed that
when the sighs and the cries escape them, they sound like
beautiful music . . . and men crowd about the poet and say
to him: "Sing for us soon again"; that is to say, May new
sufferings torment your soul.

SOREN KIERKEGAARD

No book can provide all the tools you will ever need to help your autistic clients love themselves and feel safe, but my hope is that you find this book a good place to begin. It is intended to introduce an understanding of the autistic person, not as different from others in terms of neural wiring, but instead as someone who, like a person with trauma, is in a chronic state of fight/flight and collapse. After many years there is still limited proof to support the notion that individuals with autism are differently wired, but we have a fair amount of evidence that we can better understand ourselves and our autistic clients through understanding and practicing the expressions of our autonomic nervous system.

My intent in writing this is to show not how to help autistic clients be "less autistic" but to help them manage their nervous system so they might be more mentally flexible and more socially engaged. Though that process cannot be reduced to a formula, the principle is generally simple and commonsensical, and many practical steps can be taken to address each client's goals and needs, several of which I have outlined in the chapters here. To be more connected, we need to learn to feel safer, a process that evolves with time. We can help our clients achieve this by teaching them what a sense of safety feels like and how taking deep breaths, exercising a bit more, and inviting inquiry without judgment, repeatedly and often, can help them achieve this. This is not an easy task in practice, but it is far from impossible.

This book is intended as a way to better understand our autistic clients and to prepare us to work with the broad range of clients with autism we may encounter. The overwhelming message is that the autistic client, rather than some alien pariah, is simply someone doing the best they can with what they have, operating in a frequent state of threat, usually with responses that are less-than-conscious, maladaptive attempts at protection. In this state of threat, they often have difficulty with skills that facilitate social communication—including eye contact, describing or accessing feelings, and mental flexibility—hampering their assessment of interactions and appropriate adaptive responses in the present moment.

From the lens of Polyvagal Theory, it is only through the felt sense of safety that the autistic person comes to know themselves as a deeper, more meaningful, and able person. There is a dearth of resources on this topic—this book is the first to provide such a deepened perspective on autism. My hope is that you have become inspired to continue reading and learning on this topic and, above all, that you treat your autistic clients with kindness.

GLOSSARY

ableist: building the world through the lens of people who are fully capable of carrying out most if not all functions of the human body.

adaptive information processing theory: underlying theory behind EMDR treatment protocol for trauma that describes how information is organized via bilateral stimulation.

Adult Repetitive Behavior Questionnaire-2 (ARBQ-2): psychometric tool for measuring repetitive behavior.

adverse childhood experiences (ACE): traumatic experiences in one's childhood; information about ACEs is a tool commonly used in trauma research to examine how adverse events effect health outcomes.

alexithymia: difficulty describing and labeling one's emotional experience; an external orientation of thinking.

alienation: a sense of feeling foreign to someone who should feel close and familiar.

Autism Diagnostic Interviews (ADI and ADI-R): qualitative interviews for questioning a family about the history of autism symptoms. Produced by Western Psychological Services (WPS).

Autism Diagnostic Observation Schedules (ADOS and ADOS-2): gold standard tools for measuring the phenomenon known as autism.

autonomic nervous system: made up of the ventral and dorsal vagal systems.

    dorsal vagal system: the oldest neural regulatory component of the autonomic nervous system, which evolved in very early vertebrates more than 400 million years ago. When recruited in defense, this circuit supports freeze/collapse/shutdown behaviors that involve immobilization, physical and social withdrawal, and increased rigidity—removing oneself from a perceived threat (e.g., a turtle going into its shell).

ventral vagal system: an evolutionary innovation in the autonomic nervous system that enabled nursing in modern mammals. It is an integrated social engagement system involving the ventral vagus nerve and the striated muscles of the face and head, which enable facial expressions and vocalizations in order to broadcast one's autonomic state. This system is critical in calming others through co-regulatory behaviors and it provides the neural mechanisms for humans to socially engage with others.

bilateral stimulation: action by which right and left hemispheres of the brain are stimulated during therapeutic process of EMDR.

Body Perception Questionnaire (BPQ): psychometrically valid and reliable tool used to measure hyper- and hypoarousal.

body scan: process of cultivating mindful awareness of one's body to notice what sensations are present.

cardio-inhibitory pathway: the connection between heart and breath that appears to regulate one's physiological state.

cognitive reappraisal: thinking in order to change how one thinks about a situation.

cognitive scaffolding: the developmentally necessary support one provides to allow a task to unfold while adequately supporting what a person is not yet fully capable of doing.

Deficits in Executive Functioning Scale: Russell Barkley's tool for measuring executive functioning abilities in children and adults, available from Guilford Press.

Diagnostic and Statistical Manual of Mental Disorders **(DSM)**

   DSM, fourth edition (text revision) (*DSM-4-TR*)

   DSM, fifth edition (*DSM-5*)

   DSM, fifth edition (text revision) (*DSM-5-TR*)

diaphragmatic reactivity: supra- and sub; see body perception questionnaire user manual.

dissociation: the process of leaving ones conscious awareness.

dorsal vagal system: the collapse system of the nervous system.

executive functioning (EF): a metaconstruct that covers the skills of self-management of time, self-organization/problem solving, self-restraint, self-motivation, and self-regulation of emotions.

expertise: knowledge or familiarity with a concept or topic at the level of an authority on the subject.

expressive suppression: to limit ones stated beliefs or feelings about an event, situation, or interaction.

eye movement desensitization and reprocessing (EMDR): a manualized form of adaptive information processing theory for the treatment of trauma using a protocol which involves utilizing scales to measure changes in distress of memory via use of a bilateral stimulation device or technique.

felt sense of safety: inherent feeling of ease and openness, often indicative of occupancy of the ventral vagal system.

fight-or-flight behaviors: activation of thesympathetic nervous system:

>   *fight behaviors:* physically and emotionally aggressive responses. In other mammals, this may look like biting, scratching, beating, or grasping, often in orientation to survival.

>   *flight behaviors:* physically and emotionally evasive maneuvers used to escape predators. This may look like running, swimming away, avoiding conflict, etc.

"flip the vagal switch": refers to building vagal efficiency via neural exercises.

flow: a sense of focus or loss of awareness due to engagement in some passion or interest.

freeze behaviors: collapse or freeze response; supported by the dorsal vagal system.

guiding questions hypothesis: a set possibility that can be tested and evaluated for accuracy during client interactions. This is often framed as a question, rather than a statement, given that it may or may not be an accurate representation of the possibility.

heart rate variability (HRV): A measure of the changeability of durations between successive heart beats. The more variable the durations over time, the higher the HRV, and the more consistent the beat-to-beat heart rate, the lower the HRV.

> **higher heart rate variability:** A lower heart rate and more heart rate variability are often found with states of safety or the ventral vagal state.

> **lower heart rate variability:** A higher heart rate and less rate variability are often found consistent with states of fight, flight, and collapse, in short a reflection of internal threat states supported by the dorsal vagal system and/or sympathetic nervous system.

intensity: the degree to which something is delivered, often applied to sensation or communication.

interoceptive awareness: the sense of what is happening internally in one's own body, via felt sensations.

mindfulness: present-moment awareness of one's experience.

models of disability: various perspectives that have arisen to identify, explain, assign, and address "disability" in our modern world, each with its own inherent assumptions, strengths, and limitations.

> **expertise:** The most pertinent information to apply to a particular situation. Within traditional medical models of treatment this is often within the context of a professional role (e.g., physician, nurse, behavioral analyst, psychologist). In a strengths-based medical model of psychological therapy, expertise is often shared, with each individual (including the client)—bringing to the table some knowledge that contributes to a more holistic solution to the psychological issue in question.

> **medical model of disability:** views that involve evidence-based explanations of behaviors or events (e.g., cancer) that focus on human deficits and ways to resolve these.

> **social model of disability:** the views of society on a particular phenomenon. In the context of this text, the phenomenon at hand is autism.

> **strengths perspective:** A point of view historically rooted in social work, focusing on a person's individual abilities or capacities that enhance their and often others' existences (Fung, 2021).

motivational interviewing (MI): a style of counseling involving guiding, not direction or leading, which invites changes talk rather than sustain talk.

neural exercises: clinical tools used to elicit changes in vagal efficiency. Based on research literature primarily about heart rate variability in populations both with and without autism.

neuroception: The ability to detect threat or safety in a less than conscious way.

neurodiversity: A term coined by sociologist Judy Singer in 1999 to describe how some unknown neuroanatomical or neurochemical causes people with differential wiring to behave and think differently (e.g., those with autism). Neurodiversity is considered a social model of disability.

neuroplasticity: the ability of neural networks in the brain to reorient themselves to promote growth and potentially take on new functions.

obsessive-compulsive disorder (OCD): intrusive or unwanted thoughts or impulses that reoccur outside a person's control, often generating anxiety and stress.

openness: willingness to engage in an interaction with another person or oneself.

Polyvagal Theory: a conceptualization stating that the mammalian process of neuroception to detect safety or threat works to shift one's autonomic nervous system state and promote adaptive behaviors.

posttraumatic stress disorder (PTSD): response to a terrifying or life-threatening event that results in symptoms of avoidance, emotional dysregulation, and flashbacks that lasts beyond one month.

privilege: the special rights of one group over another whether that is based on country of origin, economic conditions, race, class, etc.

respiratory sinus arrhythmia (RSA): neurophysiological measure of the speed of one's heart rate in resting and non-resting positions.

resting heart rate: heart activity when one is not under any level of stress.

role-playing: practicing a social event, often through a scripted pattern of interaction.

Role-Play Assessment of Social Skills (R-PASS): tool for the assessment of social skills.

rumination: repeated thought or focus on a specific content or interest.

Ruminative Response Scale (RRS): psychometric tool for measuring ruminative thought patterns.

Sensorimotor Psychotherapy: body-based talk therapy, developed by Pat Ogden, that focuses on 5 core organizers (the 5 senses, movement, inner sensations, cognitions, and emotions) for the resolution of trauma symptoms.

social model of disability: a disability framework that focuses on a person with a disability's strengths at the exclusion of deficits, and on the societal need for change.

social stories: developed by Carol Grey, a tool and strategy often used for capturing a concept using visual pathways.

state shifting: ability to change autonomic states. While autonomic states are changeable over time, like flipping a light switch, in some nervous systems, like those of people with autism or who have experienced trauma, they tend to be stuck in positions of threat—or in the sympathetic and dorsal vagal systems.

strengths perspective: focusing on what a client's capacities are and framing decision-making through these abilities.

sympathetic nervous system: A major regulatory component of the autonomic nervous system that evolved about 400 million years ago (prior to ventral vagus and after the dorsal vagus) and supports fight/flight strategies.

Toronto Alexithymia Scale; 20 (TAS-20): classic, gold standard tool for measuring the construct of alexithymia.

vagal efficiency: A mechanism used to describe the ability of the autonomic nervous system to return to and remain in a state of social engagement.

vagal tone: measure of how well the vagus nerve is functioning, determined by the pulse or respiratory sinus arrhythmia.

ventral vagal system: often termed the "social engagement system." Responsible for calm, socially connected actions and communication.

visceromotor psychotherapy: a clinical model of therapy in which values and neural exercises are characterized by their mindful and holistic approach Refers to the term "viscera" in "visceromotor," collectively referring to the internal organs, especially the heart, liver, and stomach. These somatic psychotherapy roots have sprouted visceromotor solutions that build on this notion that body-based changes translate into meaningful internal changes.

REFERENCES

al-Ani, M., Munir, S. M., White, M., Townend, J., & Coote, J. H. (1996). Changes in R-R variability before and after endurance training measured by power spectral analysis and by the effect of isometric muscle contraction. *European Journal of Applied Physiology and Occupational Physiology, 74*, 397–403.

Alba, G., Vila, J., Rey, B., Montoya, P., & Muñoz, M. Á. (2019). The relationship between heart rate variability and electroencephalography functional connectivity variability is associated with cognitive flexibility. *Frontiers in Human Neuroscience, 13*, 64. https://doi.org/10.3389/fnhum.2019.00064

Alderman, B. L., Olson, R. L., Brush, C. J., & Shors, T. J. (2016). MAP training: Combining meditation and aerobic exercise reduces depression and rumination while enhancing synchronized brain activity. *Translational Psychiatry, 6*(2), e726. https://doi.org/10.1038/tp.2015.225

Alderman, N., Burgess, P. W., Knight, C., & Henman, C. (2003). Ecological validity of a simplified version of the multiple errands shopping test. *Journal of the International Neuropsychological Society, 9*(1), 31–44. https://doi.org/10.1017/s1355617703910046

Ambitious about Autism. (2017). What is autism? [online] Retrieved February 10, 2020, https://www.ambitiousaboutautism.org.uk/understanding-autism/about-autism/what-is-autism

Anderson, K. A., Hemmeter, J., Rast, J. E., Roux, A. M., & Shattuck, P. T. (2020). Trends in supplemental security income payments to adults with autism. *Psychiatric Services (Washington, D.C.), 71*(6), 602–607. https://doi.org/10.1176/appi.ps.201900265

Arkowitz, H., Miller, W. R., Westra, H. A., & Rollnick, S. (2008). Motivational interviewing in the treatment of psychological problems: Conclusions and future directions. In H. Arkowitz, H. A. Westra, W. R. Miller, & S. Rollnick

(Eds.), *Motivational interviewing in the treatment of psychological problems* (pp. 324–342). Guilford Press.

Bal, E., Harden, E., Lamb, D., Van Hecke, A. V., Denver, J. W., & Porges, S. W. (2010). Emotion recognition in children with autism spectrum disorders: Relations to eye gaze and autonomic state. *Journal of Autism and Developmental Disorders*, *40*(3), 358–370. https://doi.org/10.1007/s10803-009-0884-3

Barbier, A., Chen, J. H., & Huizinga, J. D. (2022). Autism spectrum disorder in children is not associated with abnormal autonomic nervous system function: Hypothesis and theory. *Frontiers in Psychiatry*, *13*, 830234. https://doi.org/10.3389/fpsyt.2022.830234

Barkley, R. A. (2011). *Barkley deficits in executive functioning scale (BDEFS for adults)*. New York: Guilford Press.

Barkley, R. A., Knouse, L. E., & Murphy, K. R. (2011). "Correspondence and disparity in the self-and other ratings of current and childhood ADHD symptoms and impairment in adults with ADHD": Correction to Barkley et al. (2011). *Psychological Assessment*, *23*(2), 446. https://doi.org/10.1037/a0024001

Barkley, R. A., & Murphy, K. R. (2010). Impairment in occupational functioning and adult ADHD: The predictive utility of executive function (EF) ratings versus EF tests. *Archives of Clinical Neuropsychology*, *25*(3), 157–173. https://doi.org/10.1093/arclin/acq014

Barrett, S. L., Uljarevic', M., Jones, C. R. G., & Leekam, S. R. (2018). Assessing subtypes of restricted and repetitive behaviour using the Adult Repetitive Behaviour Questionnaire-2 in autistic adults. *Molecular Autism*, *9*, 58. https://doi.org/10.1186/s13229-018-0242-4

Bell, R. (2017). *How to be here: A guide to creating a life worth living*. William Collins.

Berk, L., & Winsler, A. (1995). "Vygotsky: His life and works" and "Vygotsky's approach to development." In *Scaffolding children's learning: Vygotsky and early childhood learning* (p. 24). National Association for the Education of Young Children.

Bhati, P., Shenoy, S., & Hussain, M. E. (2018). Exercise training and cardiac autonomic function in type 2 diabetes mellitus: A systematic review. *Diabetes and Metabolic Syndrome: Clinical Research and Review*, *12*, 69–78. https://doi.org/10.1016/j.dsx.2017.08.015

Brand, S., Colledge, F., Ludyga, S., Emmenegger, R., Kalak, N., Sadeghi Bahmani, D., Holsboer-Trachsler, E., Pühse, U., & Gerber, M. (2018). Acute bouts of exercising improved mood, rumination and social interaction in inpatients with mental disorders. *Frontiers in Psychology*, *9*, 249. https://doi.org/10.3389/fpsyg.2018.00249

Cabrera, A., Kolacz, J., Pailhez, G., Bulbena-Cabre, A., Bulbena, A., & Porges, S. W. (2017). Assessing body awareness and autonomic reactivity: Factor structure and psychometric properties of the Body Perception Questionnaire–Short Form (BPQ-SF). *International Journal of Methods in Psychiatric Research*, *27*(2). https://doi.org/10.1002/mpr.1596

Campbell, T. S., Labelle, L. E., Bacon, S. L., Faris, P., & Carlson, L. E. (2012). Impact of mindfulness-based stress reduction (MBSR) on attention, rumination and resting blood pressure in women with cancer: A waitlist-controlled study. *Journal of Behavioral Medicine*, *35*(3), 262–271. https://doi.org/10.1007/s10865-011-9357-1

Campbell-Sills, L., Barlow, D. H., Brown, T. A., & Hofmann, S. G. (2006). Effects of suppression and acceptance on emotional responses of individuals with anxiety and mood disorders. *Behaviour Research and Therapy*, *44*(9), 1251–1263. https://doi.org/10.1016/j.brat.2005.10.001

Carnethon, M. R., Gulati, M., & Greenland, P. (2005). Prevalence and cardiovascular disease correlates of low cardiorespiratory fitness in adolescents and adults. *JAMA*, *294*(23), 2981–2988. https://doi.org/10.1001/jama.294.23.2981

Cassidy, S. A., Gould, K., Townsend, E., Pelton, M., Robertson, A. E., & Rodgers, J. (2020). Is camouflaging autistic traits associated with suicidal thoughts and behaviours? Expanding the interpersonal psychological theory of suicide in an undergraduate student sample. *Journal of Autism and Developmental Disorders*, *50*(10), 3638–3648. https://doi.org/10.1007/s10803-019-04323-3

Classen, C. C., Hughes, L., Clark, C., Hill Mohammed, B., Woods, P., & Beckett, B. (2021). A pilot RCT of a body-oriented group therapy for complex trauma survivors: An adaptation of sensorimotor psychotherapy. *Journal of Trauma and Dissociation*, *22*(1), 52–68. https://doi.org/10.1080/15299732.2020.1760173

Colizzi, M., Sironi, E., Antonini, F., Ciceri, M. L., Bovo, C., & Zoccante, L. (2020). Psychosocial and behavioral impact of COVID-19 in autism spectrum disorder: An online parent survey. *Brain Sciences*, *10*(6), 341. https://doi.org/10.3390/brainsci10060341

Colzato, L. S., Ritter, S. M., & Steenbergen, L. (2018). Transcutaneous vagus nerve stimulation (tVNS) enhances divergent thinking. *Neuropsychologia*, *111*, 72–76. https://doi.org/10.1016/j.neuropsychologia.2018.01.003

Costandi, M. (2016). *Neuroplasticity*. MIT Press.

Cropley, M., Plans, D., Morelli, D., Sütterlin, S., Inceoglu, I., Thomas, G., & Chu, C. (2017). The association between work-related rumination and heart rate variability: A field study. *Frontiers in Human Neuroscience, 11*, 27. https://doi.org/10.3389/fnhum.2017.00027

Csíkszentmihályi, M. (n.d.). *Flow: The psychology of optimal experience.* Harper Perennial.

Cutler, C. (2018). Hell (recorded by Chelsea Cutler). On Roses.

Daanen, H. A., Lamberts, R. P., Kallen, V. L., Jin, A., & Van Meeteren, N. L. (2012). A systematic review on heart-rate recovery to monitor changes in training status in athletes. *International Journal of Sports Physiology and Performance, 7*, 251–260. https://doi.org/10.1123/ijspp.7.3.251

Dana, D. (2018). *The Polyvagal Theory in therapy: Engaging the rhythm of regulation.* Norton.

Dana, D. (2020). *Polyvagal exercises for safety and connection: 50 client-centered practices.* Norton.

Davis, K. (2015). *Meditation 101: A beginner's guide.* Narrated by D. Harris. https://www.youtube.com/watch?v=o-kMJBWk9E0

Dixon, E. M., Kamath, M. V., McCartney, N., & Fallen, E. L. (1992). Neural regulation of heart rate variability in endurance athletes and sedentary controls. *Cardiovascular Research, 26*(7), 713–719. https://doi.org/10.1093/cvr/26.7.713

Drake, K. (2022, April 19). Autism masking: What it is and more. PsychCentral. https://psychcentral.com/autism/autism-masking-why#what-is-it

Ellis, G., Voelkl, J., & Morris, C. (1994). Measurement and analysis issues with explanation of variance in daily experience using the flow model. *Journal of Leisure Research, 26*(4), 337–356. https://doi.org/10.1080/00222216.1994.11969966

Escudero-Pérez, S., León-Palacios, M. G., Úbeda-Gómez, J., Barros-Albarrán, M. D., López-Jiménez, A. M., & Perona-Garcelán, S. (2016). Dissociation and mindfulness in patients with auditory verbal hallucinations. *Journal of Trauma and Dissociation, 17*(3), 294–306. https://doi.org/10.1080/15299732.2015.1085480

Fiene, L., & Brownlow, C. (2015). Investigating interoception and body awareness in adults with and without autism spectrum disorder. *Autism Research, 8*(6), 709–716. https://doi.org/10.1002/aur.1486

Fisher, J. (2017). *Healing the fragmented selves of trauma survivors overcoming internal self-alienation.* Taylor and Francis.

Fisher, J. (2022). Working with the fragmented selves of trauma survivors: somatic and ego state techniques. PowerPoint presentation. Minnesota Society for Clinical Hypnosis.

Forte, G., Favieri, F., & Casagrande, M. (2019). Heart rate variability and cognitive function: A systematic review. *Frontiers in Neuroscience, 13,* 710. https://doi.org/10.3389/fnins.2019.00710

Fung, L. K. (2021). *Neurodiversity from phenomenology to neurobiology and enhancing technologies.* American Psychiatric Association Publishing.

Furlan, R., Piazza, S., Dell'Orto, S., Gentile, E., Cerutti, S., Pagani, M., & Malliani, A. (1993). Early and late effects of exercise and athletic training on neural mechanisms controlling heart rate. *Cardiovascular Research, 27*(3), 482–488. https://doi.org/10.1093/cvr/27.3.482

Gaus, V. L. (2018). *Cognitive-behavioral therapy for adults with autism spectrum disorder* (2nd ed.). Guilford Press.

Gray, C. (2015, November 2). What is a social story? *Social Stories.* https://carolgraysocialstories.com/social-stories/what'-is-it/

Green, R. K., Vasile, I., Bradbury, K. R., Olsen, A., Duvall, & S. W. (2022). Autism Diagnostic Observation Schedule (ADOS-2) elevations in a clinical sample of children and adolescents who do not have autism: Phenotypic profiles of false positives. *Clinical Neuropsychology, 36*(5), 943–959. https:/doi.org/10.1080/13854046.2021.1942220

Grossi, E., Caminada, E., Goffredo, M., Vescovo, B., Castrignano, T., Piscitelli, D., Valagussa, G., Franceschini, M., & Vanzulli, F. (2021). Patterns of restricted and repetitive behaviors in autism spectrum disorders: A cross-sectional video recording study. Preliminary report. *Brain Sciences, 11*(6), 678. https://doi.org/10.3390/brainsci11060678

Grossman, P., & Taylor, E. W. (2007). Toward understanding respiratory sinus arrhythmia: Relations to cardiac vagal tone, evolution and biobehavioral functions. *Biological Psychology, 74,* 263–285.

Güeita-Rodríguez, J., Ogonowska-Slodownik, A., Morgulec-Adamowicz, N., Martín-Prades, M. L., Cuenca-Zaldívar, J. N., & Palacios-Ceña, D. (2021). Effects of aquatic therapy for children with autism spectrum disorder on social competence and quality of life: A mixed methods study. *International Journal of Environmental Research and Public Health, 18*(6), 3126. https://doi.org/10.3390/ijerph18063126

Hayes, S. (n.d.) *About ACT.* Association for Contextual Behavioral Science. Retrieved February 6, 2017, from https://contextualscience.org/files/318%20 ACT%20RFT%20and%20the%20Third%20Wave%20BT%202004.pdf

Heilman, K. J., Heinrich, S., Ackermann, M., Nix, E., & Kyuchukov, H. (2023). Effects of the Safe and Sound Protocol (SSP) on sensory processing, digestive function and selective eating in children and adults with autism: A prospective single-arm study. *Journal on Developmental Disabilities.*

Heiss, S., Vaschillo, B., Vaschillo, E. G., Timko, C. A., & Hormes, J. M. (2021). Heart rate variability as a biobehavioral marker of diverse psychopathologies: A review and argument for an "ideal range." *Neuroscience and Biobehavioral Reviews, 121,* 144–155. https://doi.org/10.1016/j.neubiorev.2020.12.004

Hill, M. D. (2020). Adaptive information processing theory: Origins, principles, applications, and evidence. *Journal of Evidence-Based Social Work (2019), 17*(3), 317–331. https://doi.org/10.1080/26408066.2020.1748155

Hitchin, S. (2016). Role-played interviews with service users in preparation for social work practice: Exploring students' and service users' experience of co-produced workshops. *Social Work Education, 35*(8), 970–981. https://doi.org/ 10.1080/02615479.2016.1221393

Hodgdon, H. B., Anderson, F. G., Southwell, E., Hrubec, W., & Schwartz, R. (2022). Internal family systems (IFS) therapy for posttraumatic stress disorder (PTSD) among survivors of multiple childhood trauma: A pilot effectiveness study. *Journal of Aggression, Maltreatment and Trauma, 31*(1), 22–43. https://doi.org/10.1080/10926771.2021.2013375

Hughes, D. A. (2024). *Healing relational trauma workbook: Dyadic developmental psychotherapy in practice.* Norton.

Hwang, Y.-S., & Kearne, P. (2015). Discussion and conclusion. In *Mindfulness in behavioral health* (pp. 127–142). Springer. https://doi.org/10.1007/978-3-319 -18962-8_6

Inderbitzen, S., Gurba, A., Lerner, M., & Porges, S. W. (2023). *A polyvagal model of autism spectrum disorder: An analysis of convergent evidence from neural regulation of the autonomic nervous systems and symptomatology of autism.* Unpublished manuscript.

Inderbitzen S., & Morgan, L. (2023, January 22). Masking or camouflaging: An autistic self-advocate dialogue. *Different Brains.* https://differentbrains .org/masking-or-camouflaging-an-autistic-self-advocate-dialogue/

International OCD Foundation. (n.d.). *What is OCD?* Retrieved March 19, 2023, from https://iocdf.org/about-ocd/

Janet, P. (1925). *Principles of psychotherapy.* London: George Allen and Unwin.

Jonsdottir, S., Bouma, A., Sergeant, J. A., & Scherder, E. J. (2006). Relationships between neuropsychological measures of executive function and behavioral measures of ADHD symptoms and comorbid behavior. *Archives of Clinical Neuropsychology, 21*(5), 383–394. https://doi.org/10.1016/j.acn.2006.05.003

Jorba Galdos, L., & Warren, M. (2021). The body as cultural home: Exploring, embodying, and navigating the complexities of multiple identities. *Body, Movement and Dance in Psychotherapy, 17*(1), 81–97. https://doi.org/10.1080/17432 979.2021.1996460

Kaminsky, L. A., Arena, R., Ellingsen, Ø., Harber, M. P., Myers, J., Ozemek, C., & Ross, R. (2019). Cardiorespiratory fitness and cardiovascular disease— the past, present, and future. *Progress in Cardiovascular Diseases, 62*(2), 86–93. https://doi.org/10.1016/j.pcad.2019.01.002

Kanner, L. (1949). Problems of nosology and psychodynamics of early infantile autism. *American Journal of Orthopsychiatry, 19*(3), 416–426. https://doi. org/10.1111/j.1939-0025.1949.tb05441.x

Kinnaird, E., Stewart, C., & Tchanturia, K. (2019). Investigating alexithymia in autism: A systematic review and meta-analysis. *European Psychiatry, 55,* 80–89. https://doi.org/10.1016/j.eurpsy.2018.09.004

Kodama, S., Saito, K., Tanaka, S., Maki, M., Yachi, Y., Asumi, M., Sugawara, A., Totsuka, K., Shimano, H., Ohashi, Y., Yamada, N., & Sone, H. (2009). Cardiorespiratory fitness as a quantitative predictor of all-cause mortality and cardiovascular events in healthy men and women: A meta-analysis. *JAMA, 301*(19), 2024–2035. https://doi.org/10.1001/jama.2009.681

Kumazaki, H., Muramatsu, T., Yoshikawa, Y., Matsumoto, Y., Ishiguro, H., Mimura, M., & Kikuchi, M. (2019). Role-play-based guidance for job interviews using an android robot for individuals with autism spectrum disorders. *Frontiers in Psychiatry, 10,* 239. https://doi.org/10.3389/fpsyt.2019.00239

Kurtz, R. (2009). *Course reader on the refined Hakomi method of mindfulness-based, assisted self-discovery.* Unpublished manuscript.

Kuypers, L. (2011). *The zones of regulation.* Social Thinking Publishing.

Laborde, S., Allen, M. S., Borges, U., Iskra, M., Zammit, N., You, M., Hosang, T., Mosley, E., & Dosseville, F. (2022). Psychophysiological effects of slow-paced breathing at six cycles per minute with or without heart rate variability biofeedback. *Psychophysiology, 59*(1), e13952. https://doi.org/10.1111/ psyp.13952

Lanius, U. F., & Bergmann, U. (2014). Dissociation, EMDR, and adaptive information processing: The role of sensory stimulation and sensory awareness. In U. F. Lanius, S. L. Paulsen, & F. M. Corrigan (Eds.), *Neurobiology and treatment of traumatic dissociation: Toward an embodied self* (pp. 213–242). Springer.

Laugeson, E. A., Frankel, F., Mogil, C., & Dillon, A. R. (2009). Parent-assisted social skills training to improve friendships in teens with autism spectrum disorders. *Journal of autism and developmental disorders, 39*(4), 596–606. https://doi.org/10.1007/s10803-008-0664-5

Lee, D.-C., Sui, X., Ortega, F. B., Kim, Y. S., Church, T. S., Winett, R. A., Ekelund, U., Katzmarzyk, P. T., & Blair, S. N. (2011). Comparisons of leisure-time physical activity and cardiorespiratory fitness as predictors of all-cause mortality in men and women. *British Journal of Sports Medicine, 45*(6), 504–510. https://doi.org/10.1136/bjsm.2009.066209

Leuning, E. M., van den Berk-Smeekens, I., van Dongen-Boomsma, M., & Staal, W. G. (2023). Eye movement desensitization and reprocessing in adolescents with autism: Efficacy on ASD symptoms and stress. *Frontiers in Psychiatry, 14*, 981975. https://doi.org/10.3389/fpsyt.2023.981975

Lewis, G. F., Furman, S. A., McCool, M. F., & Porges, S. W. (2012). Statistical strategies to quantify respiratory sinus arrhythmia: Are commonly used metrics equivalent? *Biological Psychology, 89*(2), 349–364.

Liang, X., Li, R., Wong, S. H. S., Sum, R. K. W., Wang, P., Yang, B., & Sit, C. H. P. (2022). The effects of exercise interventions on executive functions in children and adolescents with autism spectrum disorder: A systematic review and meta-analysis. *Sports Medicine (Auckland, N.Z.), 52*(1), 75–88. https://doi.org/10.1007/s40279-021-01545-3

Lischke, A., Jacksteit, R., Mau-Moeller, A., Pahnke, R., Hamm, A. O., & Weippert, M. (2018). Heart rate variability is associated with psychosocial stress in distinct social domains. *Journal of Psychosomatic Research, 106*, 56–61. https://doi.org/10.1016/j.jpsychores.2018.01.005

Lobregt-van Buuren, E., Sizoo, B., Mevissen, L., & de Jongh, A. (2019). Eye movement desensitization and reprocessing (EMDR) therapy as a feasible and potential effective treatment for adults with autism spectrum disorder (ASD) and a history of adverse events. *Journal of Autism and Developmental Disorders, 49*(1), 151–164. https://doi.org/10.1007/s10803-018-3687-6

Lord, C., Risi, S., Lambrecht, L., Cook, E.H., Jr., Leventhal, B.L., DiLavore, P.C., Pickles, A., & Rutter, M. (2000). Autism Diagnostic Observation Schedule–

Generic: A standard measure of social and communication deficits associated with the spectrum of autism. *Journal of Autism & Developmental Disorders, 30*(3), 205–223.

Lord, C., Rutter, M., DiLavore, P. C., & Risi, S. (1999). *Autism spectrum disorder.* MedlinePlus. https://medlineplus.gov/genetics/condition/autism-spectrum-disorder/#:~:text=Causes&text=Changes%20in%20over%201%2C000%20genes,gene%20variations%20will%20be%20affected

Lynch, C. J., Breeden, A. L., You, X., Ludlum, R., Gaillard, W. D., Kenworthy, L., & Vaidya, C. J. (2017). Executive dysfunction in autism spectrum disorder is associated with a failure to modulate frontoparietal-insular hub architecture. *Biological Psychiatry, 2*(6), 537–545. https://doi.org/10.1016/j.bpsc.2017.03.008

Maddox, B. B., Brodkin, E. S., Calkins, M. E., Shea, K., Mullan, K., Hostager, J., Mandell, D. S., & Miller, J. S. (2017). The accuracy of the ADOS-2 in identifying autism among adults with complex psychiatric conditions. *Journal of Autism and Developmental Disorders, 47*(9), 2703–2709. https://doi.org/10.1007/s10803-017-3188-z

Mahler, K. (2016). *Comprehensive assessment for interoceptive awareness.* Autism Asperger Publishing.

Mann, T. N., Webster, C., Lamberts, R. P., & Lambert, M. I. (2014). Effect of exercise intensity on post-exercise oxygen consumption and heart rate recovery. *European Journal of Applied Physiology, 114,* 1809–1820. https://doi.org/10.1007/s00421-014-2907-9

Mayo Clinic. (2017, November 17). *Dissociative disorders.* https://www.mayoclinic.org/diseases-conditions/dissociative-disorders/symptoms-causes/syc-20355215

Mazefsky, C. A., & Oswald, D. P. (2006). The discriminative ability and diagnostic utility of the ADOS-G, ADI-R, and GARS for children in a clinical setting. *Autism, 10*(6), 533–549. https://doi.org/10.1177/1362361306068505

Mevissen, L., Ooms-Evers, M., Serra, M., de Jongh, A., & Didden, R. (2020). Feasibility and potential effectiveness of an intensive trauma-focused treatment programme for families with PTSD and mild intellectual disability. *European Journal of Psychotraumatology, 11*(1), 1777809. https://doi.org/10.1080/20008198.2020.1777809

MINT (Motivational Interviewing Network of Trainers). (n.d.). *About MINT: Motivational Interviewing Network of Trainers.* Retrieved March 20, 2023, from https://motivationalinterviewing.org/about_mint

Morgan, L. (2022, September 22). "Suicide Risk Prevention for Autistic Individuals: a Discussion with Lisa Morgan." *Uniquely Human: The Podcast.* Elevated Studio. https://uniquelyhuman.com/2022/09/29/suicide-risk-prevention-autistic-lisa-morgan/

Myers, J., Hadley, D., Oswald, U., Bruner, K., Kottman, W., Hsu, L., & Dubach, P. (2007). Effects of exercise training on heart rate recovery in patients with chronic heart failure. *American Heart Journal, 153,* 1056–1063. https://doi.org/10.1016/j.ahj.2007.02.038

Myers, J., Kokkinos, P., Chan, K., Dandekar, E., Yilmaz, B., Nagare, A., Faselis, C., & Soofi, M. (2017). Cardiorespiratory fitness and reclassification of risk for incidence of heart failure: The Veterans Exercise Testing Study. *Circulation: Heart Failure, 10*(6), e003780. https://doi.org/10.1161/CIRCHEARTFAILURE.116.003780

Nemiah, J. C., Freyberger, H., & Sifneos, P. E. (1976). Alexithymia: A view of the psychosomatic process. In O. W. Hill (Ed.), *Modern trends in psychosomatic medicine* (Vol. 3; pp. 430–439). Butterworths.

Nevill, R. E., Rey, C. N., Javed, N., Rooker, G., Yoo, H., & Zarcone, J. (2020). The development, reliability, and validity of the social impact of repetitive behavior scale in children with autism spectrum disorder. *Journal of Mental Health Research in Intellectual Disabilities, 13*(2), 127–140.

Ogden, P., Minton, K. (2000). Sensorimotor psychotherapy: One method for processing trauma. *Traumatology, 6*(3). www.fse.edu/-trauma/v6i3a3.html

Ogden, P., Minton, K., & Pain, C. (2006). Trauma and the body: A sensorimotor approach to psychotherapy. Norton.

Ogden, P., & Fisher, J. (2015). *Sensorimotor psychotherapy: Interventions for trauma and attachment.* New York: Norton.

Ogden, P. (2021). *The pocket guide to sensorimotor psychotherapy in context.* New York: Norton.

Owens, A. P., Mathias, C. J., & Iodice, V. (2021). Autonomic dysfunction in autism spectrum disorder. *Frontiers in Integrative Neuroscience, 15,* 787037. https://doi.org/10.3389/fnint.2021.787037

Pais, S. (2009). A systemic approach to the treatment of dissociative identity disorder. *Journal of Family Psychotherapy, 20*(1), 72–88. https://doi.org/10.1080/08975350802716566

Panayiotou, G., Leonidou, C., Constantinou, E., Hart, J., Rinehart, K. L., Sy, J. T., & Björgvinsson, T. (2015). Do alexithymic individuals avoid their feelings? Experiential avoidance mediates the association between alexithymia, psychosomatic, and depressive symptoms in a community and a clinical sample. *Comprehensive Psychiatry, 56*, 206–216. https://doi.org/10.1016/j.comppsych.2014.09.006

Parma, V., Cellini, N., Guy, L., McVey, A. J., Rump, K., Worley, J., Maddox, B. B., Bush, J., Bennett, A., Franklin, M., Miller, J. S., & Herrington, J. (2021). Profiles of autonomic activity in autism spectrum disorder with and without anxiety. *Journal of Autism and Developmental Disorders, 51*(12), 4459–4470. https://doi.org/10.1007/s10803-020-04862-0

Parmentier, F. B. R., García-Toro, M., García-Campayo, J., Yañez, A. M., Andrés, P., & Gili, M. (2019). Mindfulness and symptoms of depression and anxiety in the general population: The mediating roles of worry, rumination, reappraisal and suppression. *Frontiers in Psychology, 10*, 506. https://doi.org/10.3389/fpsyg.2019.00506

Patriquin, M. A., Hartwig, E. M., Friedman, B. H., Porges, S. W., & Scarpa, A. (2019). Autonomic response in autism spectrum disorder: Relationship to social and cognitive functioning. *Biological Psychology, 145*, 185–197. https://doi.org/10.1016/j.biopsycho.2019.05.004

Patriquin, M. A., Scarpa, A., Friedman, B.H., Porges, S.W. (2011). Respiratory sinus arrhythmia: A marker for positive social functioning and receptive language skills in children with autism spectrum disorders. *Developmental Psychobiology, E-pub ahead of print.* doi: 10.1002/dev.21002

Pearson, M. J., & Smart, N. A. (2018). Exercise therapy and autonomic function in heart failure patients: A systematic review and meta-analysis. *Heart Failure Reviews, 23*, 91–108. https://doi.org/10.1007/s10741-017-9662-z

Pichot, V., Roche, F., Denis, C., Garet, M., Duverney, D., Costes, F., & Barthélémy, J. C. (2005). Interval training in elderly men increases both heart rate variability and baroreflex activity. *Clinical Autonomic Research, 15*(2), 107–115. https://doi.org/10.1007/s10286-005-0251-1

Poli, A., Gemignani, A., Soldani, F., & Miccoli, M. (2021). A systematic review of a polyvagal perspective on embodied contemplative practices as promoters of cardiorespiratory coupling and traumatic stress recovery for PTSD and OCD: Research methodologies and state of the art. *International Journal of Environmental Research and Public Health, 18*(22), 11778. https://doi.org/10.3390/ijerph182211778

Polyvagal Institute. (2023). *Polyvagal Theory: Summary, premises and current status.* https://www.polyvagalinstitute.org/_files/ugd/8e115b_f8f82f01065b41d-c85e7698fd4f99818.pdf?index=true

Porges, S. W. (1976). Peripheral and neurochemical parallels of psychopathology: A psychophysiological model relating autonomic imbalance to hyperactivity, psychopathy, and autism. *Advances in Child Development and Behavior, 11*, 35–65. https://doi.org/10.1016/s0065-2407(08)60094-4

Porges, S. W. (1995). Orienting in a defensive world: Mammalian modifications of our evolutionary heritage. A Polyvagal Theory. *Psychophysiology, 32*(4), 301–318.

Porges, S. W. (2005). The vagus: A mediator of behavioral and physiologic features associated with autism. In M. L. Bauman & T. L. Kemper (Eds.), *The neurobiology of autism* (pp. 65–78). Johns Hopkins University Press.

Porges, S. W. (2009). The Polyvagal Theory: New insights into adaptive reactions of the autonomic nervous system. *Cleveland Clinic Journal of Medicine, 76*(Suppl. 2), S86–S90. https://doi.org/10.3949/ccjm.76.s2.17

Porges, S. W. (2011). *The Polyvagal Theory: Neurophysiological foundations of emotions, attachment, communication, and self-regulation.* Norton.

Porges, S. W. (2017). *The pocket guide to Polyvagal Theory: The transformative power of feeling safe.* Norton.

Porges, S. W. (2022). Heart rate variability: A personal journey. *Applied Psychophysiology and Biofeedback, 47*(4), 259–271. https://doi.org/10.1007/s10484-022-09559-x

Porges, S. W., Bazhenova, O. V., Bal, E., Carlson, N., Sorokin, Y., Heilman, K. J., Cook, E. H., & Lewis, G. F. (2014). Reducing auditory hypersensitivities in autistic spectrum disorder: Preliminary findings evaluating the listening project protocol. *Frontiers in Pediatrics, 2*, 80. https://doi.org/10.3389/fped.2014.00080

Porges, S. W., Doussard-Roosevelt, J. A., Portales, A. L., & Greenspan, S. I. (1996). Infant regulation of the vagal "brake" predicts child behavior problems: A psychobiological model of social behavior. *Developmental Psychobiology, 29*, 697–712.

Porges, S. W., Macellaio, M., Stanfill, S. D., McCue, K., Lewis, G. F., Harden, E. R., Handelman, M., Denver, J., Bazhenova, O. V., & Heilman, K. J. (2013). Respiratory sinus arrhythmia and auditory processing in autism: Modifiable deficits of an integrated social engagement system? *International Journal of Psychophysiology, 88*(3), 261–270. https://doi.org/10.1016/j.ijpsycho.2012.11.009

Prinsloo, G. E., Derman, W. E., Lambert, M. I., & Laurie Rauch, H. G. (2013). The effect of a single session of short duration biofeedback-induced deep breathing on measures of heart rate variability during laboratory-induced cognitive stress: A pilot study. *Applied Psychophysiology and Biofeedback, 38*(2), 81–90. https://doi.org/10.1007/s10484-013-9210-0

Prizant, B. M., Wetherby, A. M., Rubin, E., Laurent, A. C., & Rydell, P. J. (2006). *The SCERTS Model: Volume I: Assessment; Volume II: Program planning and intervention.* Baltimore, MD: Brookes Publishing.

Psychology Today. (n.d.). Motivational interviewing. Retrieved March 2, 2023, from https://www.psychologytoday.com/us/therapy-types/motivational-interviewing

Reuben, K., & Parish, A. (2021). *Dissociation in autism spectrum disorders: An underrecognized symptom.* Unpublished manuscript.

Robinson, J. (2017). *Enhancing the conversational skills of college students with intellectual disabilities through explicit instruction using role-play.* Unpublished manuscript.

Rosenthal, S. B., Willsey, H. R., Xu, Y., Mei, Y., Dea, J., Wang, S., Curtis, C., Sempou, E., Khokha, M. K., Chi, N. C., Willsey, A. J., Fisch, K. M., & Ideker, T. (2021). A convergent molecular network underlying autism and congenital heart disease. *Cell Systems, 12*(11), 1094–1107.e6. https://doi.org/10.1016/j.cels.2021.07.009

Ruscio, M. (2022, January 10). *What is vagal tone and how to improve yours.* Dr. Michael Ruscio DC. https://drruscio.com/vagal-tone/

Sala, R., Amet, L., Blagojevic-Stokic, N., Shattock, P., & Whiteley, P. (2020). Bridging the gap between physical health and autism spectrum disorder. *Neuropsychiatric Disease and Treatment, 16,* 1605–1618. https://doi.org/10.2147/NDT.S251394

Sandercock, G. R., Bromley, P. D., & Brodie, D. A. (2005). Effects of exercise on heart rate variability: Inferences from meta-analysis. *Medicine and Science in Sports and Exercise, 37*(3), 433–439. https://doi.org/10.1249/01.mss.0000155388.39002.9d

Santore, L. A., Gerber, A., Gioia, A. N., Bianchi, R., Talledo, F., Peris, T. S., & Lerner, M. D. (2020). Felt but not seen: Observed restricted repetitive behaviors are associated with self-report-but not parent-report-obsessive-compulsive disorder symptoms in youth with autism spectrum disorder. *Autism, 24*(4), 983–994. https://doi.org/10.1177/1362361320909177

Sargunaraj, D., Lehrer, P. M., Hochron, S. M., Rausch, L., Edelberg, R., & Porges, S. W. (1996). Cardiac rhythm effects of .125 Hz paced breathing through a resistive load: Implications for paced breathing therapy and the Polyvagal Theory. *Biofeedback and Self-Regulation, 21,* 131–147.

Schwartz, R. C. (2021). *No bad parts: Healing trauma and restoring wholeness with the internal family systems model.* Sounds True.

Sensorimotor Psychotherapy Institute. (2022, July 14). *About.* https://sensorimotorpsychotherapy.org/about/#mission

Sensorimotor Psychotherapy Institute. (2023). *Organicity.* YouTube. https://www.youtube.com/watch?v=Idu9nUrhQ3c

Shapiro, F. (2001). *Eye movement desensitization and reprocessing: Basic principles, protocols, and procedures* (2nd ed.). Guilford Press.

Shapiro F. (2014). The role of eye movement desensitization and reprocessing (EMDR) therapy in medicine: Addressing the psychological and physical symptoms stemming from adverse life experiences. *Permanente Journal, 18*(1), 71–77. https://doi.org/10.7812/TPP/13-098

Shields, G. S., Sazma, M. A., & Yonelinas, A. P. (2016). The effects of acute stress on core executive functions: A meta-analysis and comparison with cortisol. *Neuroscience and Biobehavioral Reviews, 68,* 651–668. https://doi.org/10.1016/j.neubiorev.2016.06.038

Siegel, D. J. (1999). *The developing mind: How relationships and the brain interact to shape who we are* (2nd ed.) Guilford.

Siegel, D. J. (2023). *Intraconnected: Mwe (me + we) as the integration of self, identity, and belonging.* Norton.

Silva, M. A., & Silva, D. (2017). O jogo de papéis e a criança com autismo na perspectiva histórico-cultural. *Psicologia em Estudo, 22*(3), 485. https://doi.org/10.4025/psicolestud.v22i3.35745

Singer, J. (February 1, 1999). "'Why can't you be normal for once in your life?' From a 'problem with no name' to the emergence of a new category of difference." In Corker, M., French, S. (Eds.). *Disability Discourse,* pp. 59–67. McGraw-Hill Education (UK).

Spek, A. A., van Ham, N. C., & Nyklíček, I. (2013). Mindfulness-based therapy in adults with an autism spectrum disorder: A randomized controlled trial. *Research in Developmental Disabilities, 34*(1), 246–253. https://doi.org/10.1016/j.ridd.2012.08.009

Steuwe, C., Daniels, J. K., Frewen, P. A., Densmore, M., Pannasch, S., Beblo, T., Reiss, J., & Lanius, R. A. (2014). Effect of direct eye contact in PTSD related to interpersonal trauma: An fMRI study of activation of an innate alarm system. *Social Cognitive and Affective Neuroscience, 9*(1), 88–97. https://doi.org/10.1093/scan/nss105

Streuber, S. D., Amsterdam, E. A., & Stebbins, C. L. (2006). Heart rate recovery in heart failure patients after a 12-week cardiac rehabilitation program. *American Journal of Cardiology*, *97*, 694–698. https://doi.org/10.1016/j.amjcard.2005.09.117

Tolmunen, T., Heliste, M., Lehto, S. M., Hintikka, J., Honkalampi, K., & Kauhanen, J. (2011). Stability of alexithymia in the general population: An 11-year follow-up. *Comprehensive Psychiatry*, *52*(5), 536–541. https://doi.org/10.1016/j.comppsych.2010.09.007

Treynor, W., Gonzalez, R., & Nolen-Hoeksema, S. (2003). Rumination reconsidered: A psychometric analysis. *Cognitive Therapy and Research*, *27*(3), 247–259. https://doi.org/10.1023/A:1023910315561

Trudel, C., & Nadig, A. (2019). A role-play assessment tool and drama-based social skills intervention for adults with autism or related social communication difficulties. *Dramatherapy*, *40*(1), 41–60. https://doi.org/10.1177/0263067219834712

Van Der Hart, O., Groenendijk, M., González, A., Mosquera, D., & Solomon, R. M. (2014). Dissociation of the personality and EMDR therapy in complex trauma-related disorders: Applications in phases 2 and 3 treatment. *Journal of EMDR Practice and Research*, *8*, 33–48.

Van Hecke, A. V., Lebow, J., Bal, E., Lamb, D., Harden, E., Kramer, A., Denver, J., Bazhenova, O., & Porges, S. W. (2009). Electroencephalogram and heart rate regulation to familiar and unfamiliar people in children with autism spectrum disorders. *Child Development*, *80*(4), 1118–1133. https://doi.org/10.1111/j.1467-8624.2009.01320.x

Van Hecke, A. V., Stevens, S., Carson, A. M., Karst, J. S., Dolan, B., Schohl, K., McKindles, R. J., Remmel, R., & Brockman, S. (2015). Measuring the plasticity of social approach: a randomized controlled trial of the effects of the PEERS intervention on EEG asymmetry in adolescents with autism spectrum disorders. *Journal of autism and developmental disorders*, *45*(2), 316–335. https://doi.org/10.1007/s10803-013-1883-y

Virani, S. S., Alonso, A., Benjamin, E. J., Bittencourt, M. S., Callaway, C. W., Carson, A. P., Chamberlain, A. M., Chang, A. R., Cheng, S., Delling, F. N., Djousse, L., Elkind, M. S. V., Ferguson, J. F., Fornage, M., Khan, S. S., Kissela, B. M., Knutson, K. L., Kwan, T. W., Lackland, D. T., Lewis, T. T., . . . American Heart Association Council on Epidemiology and Prevention Statistics Committee and Stroke Statistics Subcommittee. (2020). Heart disease and stroke statistics—2020 update: A report From the American Heart Association. *Circulation, 141*(9), e139–e596. https://doi.org/10.1161/CIR.0000000000000757

Virues-Ortega, J., Julio, F. M., & Pastor-Barriuso, R. (2013). The TEACCH program for children and adults with autism: a meta-analysis of intervention studies. *Clinical psychology review, 33*(8), 940–953. https://doi.org/10.1016/j.cpr.2013.07.005

Wampold, B. E., & Imel, Z. E. (2015). *The great psychotherapy debate: The evidence for what makes psychotherapy work* (2nd ed.). Routledge/Taylor and Francis Group.

Warren, S. (2022, January 13). *What is Polyvagal Theory?* Somatic Movement Center. https://somaticmovementcenter.com/what-is-polyvagal-theory/?locale=en

Weintraub, J., Cassell, D., & DePatie, T. P. (2021). Nudging flow through "SMART" goal setting to decrease stress, increase engagement, and increase performance at work. *Journal of Occupational and Organizational Psychology, 94,* 230–258.

Willcutt, E. G., Doyle, A. E., Nigg, J. T., Faraone, S. V., & Pennington, B. F. (2005). Validity of the executive function theory of attention-deficit/hyperactivity disorder: A meta-analytic review. *Biological Psychiatry, 57*(11), 1336–1346. https://doi.org/10.1016/j.biopsych.2005.02.006

Williams, D. P., Feeling, N. R., Hill, L. K., Spangler, D. P., Koenig, J., & Thayer, J. F. (2017). Resting heart rate variability, facets of rumination and trait anxiety: Implications for the perseverative cognition hypothesis. *Frontiers in Human Neuroscience, 11,* 520. https://doi.org/10.3389/fnhum.2017.00520

Williams, Z. (2021, April 22). Eight-Item General Alexithymia Factor Score (GAFS-8) calculator (based on TAS-20): GAFS-8 scoring tool. https://asd-measures.shinyapps.io/alexithymia/

Williams, Z. J., & Gotham, K. O. (2021). Improving the measurement of alexithymia in autistic adults: A psychometric investigation of the 20-item Toronto Alexithymia Scale and generation of a general alexithymia factor score using item response theory. *Molecular Autism, 12*(1), 56. https://doi.org/10.1186/s13229-021-00463-5

Williams, Z. J., McKenney, E. E., & Gotham, K. O. (2021). Investigating the structure of trait rumination in autistic adults: A network analysis. *Autism, 25*(7), 2048–2063. https://doi.org/10.1177/13623613211012855

Zainal, N. Z., Booth, S., & Huppert, F. A. (2013). The efficacy of mindfulness-based stress reduction on mental health of breast cancer patients: A meta-analysis. *Psycho-Oncology, 22*(7), 1457–1465. https://doi.org/10.1002/pon.3171

Zdankiewicz-S′cigała, E., S′cigała, D., Sikora, J., Kwaterniak, W., & Longobardi, C. (2021). Relationship between interoceptive sensibility and somatoform disorders in adults with autism spectrum traits: The mediating role of alexithymia and emotional dysregulation. *PloS One, 16*(8), e0255460. https://doi.org/10.1371/journal.pone.0255460

INDEX

ABOUT THE AUTHOR

Sean M. Inderbitzen, DSW, LCSW, an autistic psychotherapist and researcher through Mayo Clinic Health System, resides in Rice Lake, WI, with his two sons. He regularly trains healthcare professionals to be more confident when working with people on the spectrum.